Magnificent MITTENS

by anna zilboorg

photography alexis xenakis

editor elaine rowley

XRX Books would like to hear from you!

We can't publish all the knitting books in the world—only the finest. Our mission is simple: to produce quality books that rival in beauty the original knitted articles and give the reader skill-building instructions and confidence.

Because we care about books, we are attracting the best authors in the knitting universe: Priscilla Gibson-Roberts, Anna Zilboorg, Meg Swansen, Sally Melville, and Shirl the Purl are just a few of the experts who have found at XRX Books a passion for knitting and a commitment to quality. And our use of cutting-edge computer technology means we can spend more time editing and designing: our Editor can upload files in South Dakota one minute to be downloaded by our Knitting Editor in New York and Technical Editor in Nebraska the next.

You are the reason for XRX Books, and we would very much like to hear your comments, suggestions, and ideas for improvement. You may reach us in a variety of ways:

by mail
XRX Books
PO Box 1525
Sioux Falls, South Dakota
57101-1525

by phone
605.338.2450

by fax
605.338.2994

by eMail
rowley.elaine@xrx-inc.com

You may also visit our XRX Books site on the World Wide Web: xrx-inc.com

Or join in the conversation
and post your reactions in our book discussion area: xrx-inc.com/cgi-bin/kniTalk

We very much look forward to hearing from you.

AN XRX BOOK

PUBLISHER Alexis Yiórgos Xenakis

EDITOR Elaine Rowley

KNITTING EDITOR Ann Regis

STYLIST Nancy J. Thomas

PHOTOGRAPHER Alexis Yiórgos Xenakis

DIGITAL CONSULTANT David Xenakis

GRAPHIC DESIGNER Mark Sampson

PRODUCTION Carol Skallerud CHIEF
Jay Reeve
Patrick McGowan

MARKETING DIRECTOR Benjamin Xenakis

FIRST PUBLISHED IN USA IN 1998 BY XRX, INC.
PO BOX 1525, SIOUX FALLS, SD 57101-1525

COPYRIGHT © XRX, INC. 1998

LIBRARY OF CONGRESS
CATALOG CARD NUMBER: 97-62549

ISBN 0-9646391-3-0

Produced in Sioux Falls, South Dakota by XRX, Inc., 605.338.2450

Color separations by Digital Imaging, Sioux Falls, South Dakota

Printed in Hong Kong

acknowledgements

My thanks to all who have admired my mittens, bought them, and worn them. Their enthusiasm stands at the base of this book. I am also endlessly grateful to Priscilla Gibson-Roberts who has befriended and encouraged me, and to a large extent caused this book to be written.

Though it seems a little redundant to thank XRX, they are those without whom this book would not be. Alexis' photographs speak for themselves. Elaine does not speak for herself, but she worked hardest and longest to make this book useful for all knitters. And Carol, who drew the illustrations, was impressive and wonderful to work with. On top of the technical support, the friendliness of the whole crew made work into play.

Finally, I want to thank David Oliver who patiently instructed me on how to use a computer so that I could write this book. It was a painful job because of my petulant ineptitude and continual complaints. He deserves better. Mittens at least.

for Arianne
who encourages me
even to sing

epigraph

Where love is concerned small things become important. For real love is too infinite ever to be adequately expressed in its greatness; and so we reverse the attempt and symbolize it by infinitesimal actions and attentions—things that prove love because they are too slight for anything but love to think worth doing, as for anything but love to see when done.   —Dr. Illingworth

contents

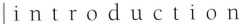

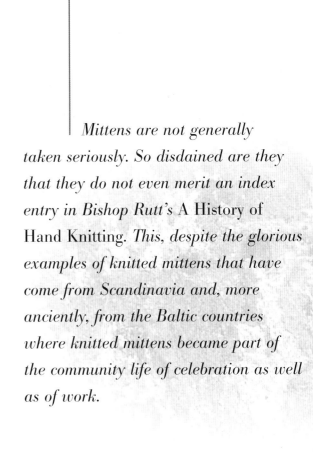

Mittens are not generally taken seriously. So disdained are they that they do not even merit an index entry in Bishop Rutt's A History of Hand Knitting. *This, despite the glorious examples of knitted mittens that have come from Scandinavia and, more anciently, from the Baltic countries where knitted mittens became part of the community life of celebration as well as of work.*

How I wish this were the case in the modern world! And why should it not be? Knitting is a craft that all harried people—and who is not harried today?—can benefit by practicing. Mittens are a small enough project that they should not daunt even slow knitters. That two are necessary might give some pause. But there's really no need to repeat. Reverse the colors on the second mitten, or change the pattern and leave the colors alone. They'll still be a pair.

It can be argued, of course, that mittens have no place in contemporary life. Alas, this is true. But it need not remain so. All that is necessary is that individuals knit wonderful mittens and wear them anywhere and everywhere. Indeed, I have made evening mittens (see pattern 5-8, p. 82), patterned in gold. They were bought by a very elegant lady.

The only practical drawback I know to mittens in the modern

world, is that everyone must drive automobiles and knitted fabric slips on the steering wheel. This is undeniable. One can either cover the steering wheel or sew a strip of leather or ultra-suede (see p. 16) where you need them to grip.

The advantages of mittens far outweigh the one drawback. Especially if they are lined in angora or alpaca or kid mohair—as I think all mittens deserve to be—they are not only cozy and warm in the worst of weather, but wearing them is itself a sensual experience. (I remember one woman who came into my booth at a craft show with the single firm intention of buying a hat for her daughter. She tried on a mitten. The sensation so overcame her maternal feelings that she bought the mittens instead of the hat. Though she lamented her lack of discipline, she felt she had no choice.)

Furthermore—I return to this again and again—mittens are beautiful on everyone. You don't have to be a special size or shape to look your best in them. If they're showy enough, they will draw attention away from any less attractive features you may have. The shape of mittens is innately pleasing. The making of them is a delight.

I've had a wonderful time making the mittens in this book. You can reproduce them exactly if you like—same yarn, same colors (see Dyes and Kits, p. 136), but there's certainly no need to do that. Your own favorite colors will make any pattern your own. Beyond that, there are blank charts that you can photocopy as often as you like and fill in with your own patterns or any mixture of any others.

There's an American tradition for this kind of social craft: quilting. Quilts use traditional patterns and are pieced of all kinds of cloth and all kinds of colors. They end up individual and various, cherished and useful. Their drawbacks are that they aren't knitting and that they take an enormous amount of time to finish.

Try mittens.

1 | n o t e s   a n d   c o m m e n t s

The directions

The instructions I give are for knitting mittens from the fingertips down to the wrist. This is opposite from the way most mittens are made. I find it far more pleasant and satisfying than the other direction. Indeed, I tried mittens once and quit because they were not fun to do: I found adding on the thumb after finishing the mitten was awkward and unrewarding. Any aesthetic impulse to try again was undermined by the shaping at the tip. It always seemed to compromise the pattern. When, however, I discovered Turkish socks and their toe beginning, a new world of mittens opened up for me. The thumb is done separately—not as clumsy an operation as doing it with a mitten hanging down. The pattern is designed from the tip down so it fits the shaping perfectly. Further, there is a narrow band that goes from wrist to wrist over the top of the mitten—an elegant designing frame.

In addition, and very importantly, there is the actual technique of beginning at the tip. It's awkward to do when you first try, but it's a lot of fun and truly satisfying when you see it working out. It is, as a student remarked looking at her one inch tip, "way cool." So that is why I knit my mittens from the top. I encourage everyone to give it a try.

In the course of these directions, I find myself commenting over and over on whether a pattern is difficult or easy, boring or fun. I do so because I find these criteria really important in deciding whether I want to make something or not. In different moods, I may want something challenging or simple-minded, however I never want to be bored; I want to enjoy what I'm doing. The problem with making judgements is that what I experience one way, another may experience totally differently. So you should not trust me over much.

Designations of difficulty and what makes a pattern fun might need a little explanation, especially as one editor, looking at my remarks, wondered what they were all about. She felt you just moved an index card up the chart and followed the row. I guess many people knit this way, but I think if I had to, I'd never knit another pattern. I like to watch my knitting, not a chart, and to feel a rhythm in the alternation of colors that makes the pattern almost a dance.

So when I say a pattern is simple, I mean that you can tell what the next round will be just looking at the previous one. When easy, I mean you can learn how to do it without having to look at the chart after you've been through one or two repeats. The patterns I find most fun are those that alternate colors in a pleasing way. I don't tend to think about main color and pattern color. Since there are only two colors, I only think of the alternations. Thus, a run of 21 stitches might appear on a chart as: OOOOOXXXOXXXOXXXOOOOO. I would read that as 5-3, 1-3, 1-3, 5. Or I might read it as: 5-3-1, 3, 1-3-5. In any case those numbers would be the number of stitches of one color and then the number of stitches of the other color. I do not have to count five O's, knit them, look at the chart, count three X's etc.

If I have a pattern that I cannot do by turning a row into a rhythm I can follow, and cannot learn to follow without the chart, I consider it a difficult pattern—a very difficult pattern indeed. If I'm up for a challenge, I may do it. If I want something undemanding, I won't. Fortunately for us who are indolent and self-indulgent, many of the most beautiful knitting patterns are also the easiest.

Most of my mittens have very large cuffs. I do this for aesthetics, but also to prevent snow and wind from getting up your sleeves. This is an advantage not to be overlooked.

Mitten shapes

When mittens were made of woven cloth or leather, it was necessary to use gussets and shaping to make them fit at all. When Scandinavians started knitting them, they followed the sewn patterns far more than was necessary for comfort.

The mittens that I am presenting here are easier and quicker, though I do not want them to be less beautiful. So I am using, for the majority of the mittens, an even older shaping that

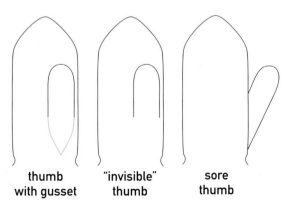

thumb with gusset   "invisible" thumb   sore thumb

comes from the Baltic region. Here the thumb is placed on the the palm with no gusset shaping. It is patterned to match the palm of the mitten. I have called these mittens "Invisible-Thumb Mittens." When they are done with fine yarn and needles, the thumb virtually disappears against the palm. At my coarser gauge, the thumb is more visible. Nevertheless, I find matching the thumb this way is elegant and appealing. The invisible thumb does not fit the hand exactly, but knitting is generous and I have never heard anyone complain of serious discomfort wearing an invisible-thumb mitten. The advantages of the invisible thumb are ease of working and, to my eye at least, a more aesthetically pleasing finished object.

On the other hand, I would like to accommodate those who prefer gussetted thumbs, so I have made some patterns for them. In *Knitter's Almanac*, Elizabeth Zimmermann declared that there was no need to place a gusset on the palm, thereby distinguishing the right and left-hand mittens. She said the gussets should stick straight out from the side so that mittens could be worn on either hand. Since her word is law to me, this is the way I have designed the mittens and have named them "Sore-Thumb Mittens," because the thumb sticks out like one. They have the aesthetic advantage that you can make the band go continuously around the edge of the hand and over the thumb.

Any invisible-thumb mitten can be made with a sore thumb. Draw the pattern you want using the blank sore-thumb chart (p. 138), and insert it in place of the invisible thumb. You could also turn a sore-thumb mitten into an invisible one, but with these patterns it would be ungainly: you would have to, on most of them, include some of the band pattern in the thumb. Otherwise the thumb would come too far into the palm. An invisible thumb should not be more than a stitch or two from the side of the mitten. (All these distinctions should be a lot clearer from looking at some examples in the book.)

Materials

For warmth and wear, mittens should be worked at a somewhat tighter gauge than you would normally use. Stranded knitting tends to work up half a stitch to an inch tighter anyway, so you may not have to use a smaller needle than usual. I use "Texas" a DK-weight, mohair and wool combination from Henry's Attic. It runs about 60 yards to an ounce, but it is smooth and fairly tightly spun and can be knit at 6 to 6½ stitches to the inch (the gauge of my mittens).

Then there's the question of fiber. Actually, there's no question at all: mittens should be made in wool. People who are allergic to wool should do without knitted mittens. I'm sorry to say this because I'm sorry to think of anyone without knitted mittens, but it is true. Mittens are worn for warmth as well as beauty. It isn't easy to keep hands warm, hence the warmest materials are necessary. Wool is the fiber—especially since it stays warm even when wet. (I didn't quite believe

this until I was hiking in a deluge one time. My boots had so much water in them that it bubbled up between my toes at every step. But my socks were wool and that water got warm and stayed warm.)

Stranded mittens give two layers of wool so there are lots of air spaces to provide good insulation. Nevertheless, for the warmest mittens, you'll want to line them. Since you're putting so much labor and love into them anyway, and they'll be so beautiful, you might as well use the best lining material. This is either angora or alpaca, or even kid mohair. (Do not use acrylic. Even fluffy acrylic that looks and feels like angora. It just does not work for warmth.) All these are worked up loosely, so the lining doesn't take forever to do, and they fluff up to provide the best possible insulation. With time the lining felts into the mitten a bit making them virtually waterproof and windproof.

There is one more advantage to lining mittens: There is no need to finish off ends on the inside. Just clip them to about an inch and let them hang. This may not be important to many people, but it is to some.

I dye my own colors using ProChemical's washfast acid dyes. I've given the recipes for all the colors I've used in Chapter 10 (p. 136). They'll be clear to anyone who is accustomed to dyeing except for the designation "toner," the recipe for which also appears there. People who dye are generally so fond of their own colors that I doubt they would be using my recipes. Still, someone who is about to plunge into dyeing might be encouraged by having a few recipes to start out with. If so, it will have been worthwhile printing them all.

To start knitting from the fingertip down, it's much easier to have short needles. I find some of the tiny 3" "finger pins" just too short. At this writing, Brittany has begun making 4¾" birch double pointed needles (dpn). They are smooth, the points finely tapered, and I find them just about perfect. I expect the finish will wear off with time but I'm hoping a little wax will restore them. If you are going to do the whole mitten on four needles (knitting with the fifth), and are arranging the stitches so that each holds one quarter of the mitten, the Brittany needles are all you will need. That is, there is no necessity for having 7" or 8" dpns as well. Of course some people would rather work with long dpns—I'm just not one of them. By all means suit yourself.

The other needle that might be useful is the 11½" or 12" circular needle. They take some getting used to and many people can't be bothered. I love them—but not all of them. The Susan Bates needles I've found wonderful. Now I hear they've stopped making them. Addi turbo needles have a 12" that I also like a lot, but it's a little stiffer and hence harder to use when decreasing, binding off, or picking up stitches. You can always use one of your dpn for these operations, however, and the circular needle, once you're used to it, makes the knitting zip along pleasantly.

Patterns and designing

As you will see, the general directions for these mittens are separated from their charts (pp. 26–33). This was an editorial decision based largely on aesthetics: it seemed both ugly and unnecessary to fill pages with repeated directions and be forced to scale down the charts to a miserably small size. To get the charts and directions side by side for working purposes, you could photocopy one or the other and use the photocopied sheet as a bookmark.

You can reproduce the mittens in this book if you want, but I would urge you not to. In the directions I've mentioned some that are particularly good as scrap mittens, that is, they invite you to use leftover bits and pieces from other projects. But not only the ones I've marked can be done that way. Large overall designs take on a whole new character if you begin them with one color and change it as you go. If the ground color remains the same, the pattern will keep its integrity, and if you like the look of each new color against what is already there, the whole cannot help but be pleasing. It doesn't matter if you run out of a color on a pair of mittens. If the pattern is the same in both, the colors can be as varied as you like or have scraps for. On the other hand, if you come up with a strong color combination, you can have different patterns on each mitten and they'll still read as a pair. (This would also let you tell right from left at a glance.)

If you want to try out colors on paper before plunging into the knitting, photocopy the chart (or charts) and color them in with markers or colored pencils. This is especially useful if you like different parts of cuff designs and want to know how they would look together. Color, cut, and paste.

In addition to changing colors, you can vary textures. A pattern worked in a looped yarn will look very different from the same pattern in a smooth yarn. Just as surely, you can make any cuff to go with any mitten and any finish to go on any cuff. The attitude I'd like to encourage is that if you like it, it's right. If it doesn't look quite right to you, add something—and something else—until it does please you. You are the only one who needs pleasing here: these are mittens, after all.

Designing your own mittens from scratch should be easy after perusing this book. All you need is a blank chart with a mitten outline into which you fit your own pattern. There are blank charts given in the back of this book that can be photocopied and used over and over (pp. 138–139). You should not feel limited to patterns that already have the correct number of stitches. Often a few alterations will make something fit that would not at first glance. Also, you should freely take pieces of patterns that appeal to you and use them in different ways. (I've made some remarks about this under particular mittens that I've designed that way.) You'll want to look out

for how long the carries are when you're fitting a pattern onto a chart, because too many too long, especially on the tip and the thumb, make for unpleasant knitting. Also watch for how long the mitten has to be and where the pattern ends. If the pattern doesn't fit well lengthwise as well as crosswise, it may not look well.

When I'm working on a new pattern, I usually copy the whole thing out several times. Not that I want to particularly, but I have to keep changing things to get it right. Copying the whole thing over is often easier than erasing, and in the process of copying, I really get to know the pattern. When it comes to knitting it, the fore-knowledge is very helpful.

I don't think about the thumb until I get there. That is, when I put in my hand and the mitten reaches the crotch of my thumb. Then I mark the row I've just done on my chart. With my hand in the mitten, I see where the tip of my thumb comes and mark that row. Next I draw a vertical line on my chart joining those two rows a stitch or two short of half way across the chart. There. I have a chart for my thumb. If a pattern repeat will fit evenly into the number of thumb stitches necessary, the vertical line is not necessary (see Chapter 3, Small-patterned mittens, pp. 34–65). On some complicated patterns it is worthwhile marking the center of the thumb chart with a highlighting pen. Then each needle of the thumb can be easily read. Highlighters are good for other markings as well, such as color changes.

I use 8-squares-per-inch graph paper, not knitters' graph paper. With stranded knitting most people get almost as many rows per inch as stitches per inch. If that is not true for you, you might want to try larger needles, which will affect the row gauge more than the stitch gauge. Of course there's nothing wrong with any gauge, but most of my patterns look better when the stitch and row gauge are close to the same. I avoid fine quality vellum graph paper because it smudges and it's so transparent that it's hard to see what you are doing, especially if you're working lightly with pencil—which I always do.

I use a mechanical pencil and a mechanical eraser that looks like a pencil and is much the same size. This is more important than it might seem. When one is drawing one uses an eraser just as much as a pencil. A miserable little eraser stuck at the end of the pencil makes people feel as though they have done something wrong every time they use it. Nothing could be more inhibiting. I know. I never designed anything for a large part of my life because it wasn't any fun at all; it just made me feel bad. A positive relationship with your eraser can make a big difference. Then it's an adventure to try things. When they look horrible, it's a discovery. Designing is a joyful journey into an unknown. One caveat may be worthwhile. It takes a lot of time. It takes more time than you ever thought it possibly could. Undertake a design instead of an evening of television or the movies. You might have a mitten at the end, or you might not, but I hope you will have had a fine time.

Designing the cuff is another matter. I usually have an idea of what kind of cuff I want when I start a mitten but I've learned better than to spend a lot of time working out a careful design. More often than not, when I get to the wrist and look at what I actually have, I want a different cuff than I'd imagined. The same is true for the finishing edges. There's nothing wrong with a few ridges of garter stitch or a few rounds of ribbing, but there are a lot of other fine possibilities. I've done some; I'm sure others can come up with many more. No one should be limited by my limitations!

Sizing

There's a lot of flexibility in sizing mittens. With only 54 or 56 stitches around most adult mittens, exact gauge is not critical. Anywhere between 6 and 6½ stitches to the inch will make them an average woman's size (measuring approximately 8½–9" around).

To make them larger, use a yarn that will knit up firmly at 5–5½ stitches to the inch (for a mitten measuring 10–11" around). To make them smaller, knit at 7–7½ stitches to the inch (for a mitten measuring 7½–8" around). (Since stranded knitting tends to be a bit tighter than single layer knitting, the yarns that give these gauges are worsted weight and sport yarn. Examples are Classic Elite's Tapestry and Norsk Finnulgarn.)

Two of the mittens have been made for a small child, approximately three to five years old. To make them larger or smaller, change the yarns as above. One mitten is man-sized. It can be made smaller by omitting four stitches front and back (this is indicated in the pattern) or by changing gauge.

There are times, however, when one wants to change the size without changing the yarn and hence the weight. 4 stitches will make a substantial difference. To add 4 stitches, you will usually want to add one more stitch on each side of the back and palm. For most patterns this presents no problem, though you'll probably want to make a new chart with the stitches added. It will be easier to follow in the long run. If you want to add a stitch to each side of the band, that's also possible, but you should not place the thumb all the way inside the band in that case. Include the extra band stitch in the thumb chart. Or you could make them into sore-thumb mittens.

When you want to make a pattern smaller, particularly to make a child's mitten from an adult pattern, it will be necessary to fit the desired pattern into a new chart. Sometimes you also just want to make new patterns, whether from pieces of others or different entirely. To facilitate this, blank charts follow for average women's, small and medium children's, and men's mittens (pp. 138–139). I urge everyone to photocopy a chart or two and fill them in with whatever patterns or combination of patterns please you. Decide whether to use a plain or striped band by how long the carries are on the sides of the pattern, and follow the general directions. There is nothing magic in my designs; the blank chart will work for anything that fits into it.

In designing a cuff, anything goes. For a cuff large enough to go over the sleeve of a coat, you'll probably want it to be 7" long and about 100 stitches by the time it is finished. Decide which patterns you want to knit and increase stitches before and between them, usually in three places. Sometimes you will want to increase within the pattern (see mitten 4-7, p. 49 and 5-11, p. 89).

The knitting itself

Once the increases are made for the tip of the mitten, there are really few problems and little advice to give. The only helpful advice I can think of for the tip is patience. When you're asking fingers to do unusual things, it often takes them awhile to figure out how—even when your head gives careful instructions. Once they learn they never forget.

There is one other thing that can be said about new techniques: written directions are very hard to learn from. Knitting instructions never used to be written and read, they weren't even spoken and listened to; they were demonstrated and copied. This is still the easiest way to learn a new technique. I've tried to be as clear in writing as possible, but even there, what is clear to one may be murky to another. I believe the drawings are the next best thing to having someone demonstrate. Work slowly and don't panic. Nothing in knitting is that hard!

On the first few rounds there are times when the pattern or ground color is not used on the band so it carries across the knitting instead of going around it. Don't worry about it: the distances are small enough that the carry won't pull unless you really make it tight—which, of course, you know better than to do. When you have completed the increases you have many stitches on two needles and few on two other needles. It's perfectly possible to continue knitting this way but it's probably more comfortable to move the stitches around. Work the band stitches plus half the mitten stitches on one needle, the other half of the mitten stitches on the next needle. Repeat for the other side of the mitten. I arrange the stitches this way before I switch to a short (12") circular needle because it makes it easier.

A few words about the thumb itself. It is not altogether enjoyable for most people to knit a thumb-sized tube in two or more colors, following an often-difficult chart, just to match the palm pattern exactly. The temptation exists to knit the thumb plain. I would urge you to stand against it: the thumb, even more than the fingers (which have each other) needs the double layer of knitting for warmth. If the charted pattern is too cheerless a prospect, use a simple unrelated pattern, such as a 2x2 check or

1 x 1 stripes

2 x 2 checks

1x1 stripes. It's only for a couple of inches and in addition to being warmer, any pattern will look better than none.

Of the ways one can attach the thumb to the mitten, I prefer the one that knits together thumb and palm stitches before knitting any further. This is because I like to have as much finished when I bind off as possible. Knitting the thumb to palm involves a lot of needle points in all directions getting in the way if your mitten stitches are not on a holding thread. I've finally figured a way out of this, though many people would find it more trouble than it's worth. But I like it. Do this: place the thumb stitches on two needles, front and back. Place the mitten stitches on two needles, palm and back. Then line up the thumb stitches with the matching palm stitches and cast them off together. The other thumb stitches and the other mitten stitches stay neatly out of the way.

Usually the patterns call for reducing stitches at the wrist, working a few rounds, and then increasing to begin the cuff. Most of the cuff patterns will look best if the pattern is centered on the back of the hand. This is not difficult to do. Find the center stitch on the back of the mitten. Follow it to the corresponding stitch on the needle. Count back from that stitch half the number of stitches in the cuff pattern (if the cuff pat is 10 stitches, count back 5 stitches). Begin your round there. If this is an awkward place to begin the round (a jog will show on the back of the hand), count back another pattern's worth of stitches (in the above example, count back 5 + 10 stitches or even 5 + 20 stitches).

Finishing

If you are going to line your mittens, you don't have to run in the yarn ends. I generally run them in on the thumb and at its base to make the thumb neater. There will be holes at each side of the thumb where it has joined to the mitten. The best way to deal with these is to turn the mitten inside out and work with the yarn tails. Thread the end on your darning needle and run it through purl bumps on the wrong side all around the hole—twice if the hole seems large. Pull it up. It should close nicely and be quite invisible from the right side. The ends on the cuff should be finished. Just skim the darning needle through the double thickness of knitting for an inch or two and cut off the end.

Little if any blocking is required. Steaming, however, never hurts.

Sewing on a leather or other non-slipping palm is simple, though not particularly attractive. There is a minimalist solution (I use this one myself): cut a strip of leather, or leather substitute, about an inch wide and five inches long. Sew or fabric glue it on the inside of the thumb and up the palm. This will give non-slip grip on a steering wheel and not interfere too much with the mitten pattern.

Possibilities for palms other than leather that are easily available in fabric stores are ultrasuede (very elegant, but I don't know how well it wears—possibly very well) or one of the various vinyls.

Mittens from the bottom up

There probably are mitten knitters in the world who love to knit mittens from cuff to tip. Even after open-mindedly trying a pair from the top down, they may still prefer their old way of doing it. It is for these knitters that this section is written.

All of these patterns can be worked from cuff to tip. For the most part there is no problem involved; you simply follow the directions backwards. After working your cuff of choice from the top of the graph down, decreasing where the directions call for increasing, you move on to the mitten, increasing instead of decreasing and working the chart in reverse. The first deviation comes when you reach the thumb.

For invisible-thumb mittens: Mark on the chart where the thumb will be inserted. (If you are following my generalized fitting, that is already marked.) When you reach that place, put the marked stitches on two needles. Cast on identical stitches on two more needles and work around the thumb following the chart until it is long enough to fit your thumb. With the background color, knit two stitches together around, knit one round, knit two stitches together around again and draw the stitches together with the tail and a darning needle. Now return to the mitten proper, pick up stitches in pattern at the base of the thumb and continue up the hand.

If you prefer, you can work the thumb after finishing the hand. Remove the thumb stitches onto a holding thread at the base of the thumb. Then cast on identical stitches and continue knitting up the hand. When the mitten is finished, return to the thumb. Put the stitches on the thread on two needles. Pick up stitches in pattern at the base of your cast-on stitches and continue up the thumb following the chart as far as you want.

The sore-thumb mittens would be worked essentially the same way except that you would be casting on fewer stitches for the hand than you would be removing for the thumb, and you would have been increasing, following the chart, from wrist to thumb.

The shaping at the tip involves once again decreasing instead of increasing. On the right side of each band you knit together the last stitch of the mitten and the first stitch of the band. On the left side of the band you ssk with the last stitch of the band and the first stitch of the mitten. When you come to the end of the chart and there are three stitches left on front and back, work back and forth on one band, decreasing at the end of each row until there are no more stitches on front and back. Now graft together the band stitches. If you are not a perfectionist, you may want to just graft together the band stitches and the other stitches. As long as you place the band stitches together, it really won't show.

That's all I can think of saying about these mittens. I hope you enjoy them and that they inspire you to make something wonderful!

2 | beginner's mittens

This chapter is for those who know how to knit but have rarely (or never) knit with four or five needles and have never (or rarely) knit with two colors. There are techniques for the mittens in this book that may well be unfamiliar to experienced knitters. They need not read through this whole chapter since the general directions include detailed instructions. Less experienced knitters can work through these beginning mittens with growing confidence and skill so that they are not afraid to take on any pattern in the book, or to plunge in and design their own.

Before picking up needles, I want to say a few words about these techniques and the learning of them. First of all, stranded knitting (knitting with two colors) is not difficult. This is true despite all the published patterns that say multicolored patterns are for experts. Following charts can be difficult if they are complicated and you must refer to them constantly. (I've commented throughout this book on which patterns are easy to learn and which are difficult to follow.) But the actual technique of using two colors is absolutely simple—provided you are going around in a circle.

That brings up knitting with four or five double pointed needles (dpn). These enable you to knit around in a circle when you have too few stitches to use a circular needle. Most Western-style small circular knitting (mittens, gloves, and socks) is done with stitches on three double-pointed needles, worked with a fourth. Every time you knit across a needleful of stitches, you liberate that needle to use knitting the next needleful. Other traditions use four needles, working with a fifth. Though this means changing needles one more time to get around once, it is in fact easier to have four needles with stitches than three. The piece lies flat (in half) while you're knitting so it feels more like knitting with straight needles. When you try it, I think you'll agree that the needles feel better in the hand when there are four. Don't take my word for it; try them both. Then do as you choose.

The reason that circular knitting makes stranded knitting easy is two-fold. First, there is no purling. That means the yarn is always away from the piece so you can see what you're doing. Since the right side is always toward you, you can see the pattern and more easily avoid being bound to the chart and making mistakes. Second, since you are always knitting in the same direction, the yarns are not getting tangled. This is especially true if you are knitting with one yarn in each hand—but that's jumping ahead.

About learning, there is one thing to say: it isn't easy. It is always difficult for fingers to learn to do something new. On the other hand, when they do, they learn it. They never forget it, unlike the mind which learns easily and forgets quickly. People lose confidence, feel they cannot do something, because their minds understand what is required but their fingers haven't gotten it yet. What is needed is patience, perseverance, and kindness. Talk to your fingers as you would to a dog you were trying to train to sit up while he was sure you meant roll over. They'll catch on and you'll be delighted.

The best way to learn a new technique is from a person beside you, showing you every movement. But this is a book. I cannot see where your hands are having trouble or where my directions are obscure. If you can enlist human help, by all means do so. If not, relax, take your time. This isn't a contest or a trial. It's a doorway to a whole new ability. Furthermore, none of these techniques are inherently difficult. There are some things one can learn to do that never become easy (knitting three together comes to mind: utterly simple to understand, never much fun to do). Stranded and circular knitting, once learned, are easy, fun, and almost never boring.

To begin

Equip yourself with two colors of a yarn that knits up to about 6 stitches to one inch—a heavy sport yarn or light double knitting (dk) yarn, nothing that splits easily or tangles—you will use one color as the main color (MC) and the other as the contrast color (CC). It takes about five yards of contrast color yarn to work this color pattern, so you might use several leftovers on these mittens, as I have. Get a set of five short double pointed needles appropriate for the yarn. At this writing Brittany makes 4¾" wooden sets. They have excellent points and the stitches do not easily slide off the needles. I highly recommend them. If, however, you are a very tight knitter, you may find the stitches slide more easily on Inox's 6" aluminum needles. The very short (3") finger pins made by some other companies are fine for thumbs but really too short for mittens.

Figure-8 cast-on

Place two needles together horizontally. Hold the MC yarn against them with your left thumb (left index finger is on the other side of the needles). Leave a 5" tail of yarn. Take the yarn attached to the ball in your right hand. **To make a figure-8 wrap**: Bring the yarn between the needles to the back, over the top needle to the front, then between the needles to the back again, then under the bottom needle to the front, and through the middle to the back: one figure-8 wrap made, one loop on the top needle and one on the bottom needle. Repeat until you have four wraps on the top needle and four wraps on the bottom needle (Fig. 1).

Now you start to knit. Anchoring the tail yarn with your left thumb, push the top needle back until the loops are near the tip (Fig 2). Take another needle and knit the four loops off the top needle. Hold the tail in front, turn and purl back (when you turn, the tail is then in the back; Fig 3). Drop the yarn.

Turn work and rotate the needles so that the unknit loops are on top and the tail is on your right. The loops are loose. Using the 3rd needle, pull the loops tight, one by one. Begin pulling the loop 2nd from the

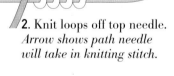

1. Figure-8 cast-on.
Shaded yarn is the tail yarn, unshaded yarn is the ball yarn.

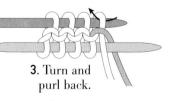

2. Knit loops off top needle.
Arrow shows path needle will take in knitting stitch.

3. Turn and purl back.

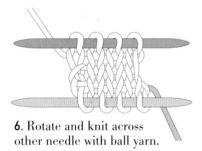

4. Turn work and rotate so unknit loops are at top and tighten them, working from left to right. *Drawing shows two stitches tightened and needle in last stitch adjusting third stitch.*

5. With the tail of yarn, knit into the back loops of these four stitches.

6. Rotate and knit across other needle with ball yarn.

7. Pick up and knit three stitches along edge.

Shading indicates 2½ stitches that will be seen as the band of the mitten.

left. Pull each one to the right and end by pulling the tail (Fig 4). Now with the tail yarn, knit through the back of the loops across the four stitches (Fig 5).

Rotate the whole piece clockwise until the other needle is on top and the yarn attached to the ball is on the right. Knit across the four stitches (Fig 6). You have a small rectangle with stitches on two sides.

To knit around the rectangle: Take a free needle. Pick up and knit three stitches on the side of the rectangle. Follow the stitch placement indicated by the arrows on Fig 7. With a free needle, knit across the next four stitches (Fig. 8). Then, with another free needle, pick up three stitches on the other side of the rectangle (Fig 9). With the last free needle, knit across the four stitches on next needle.

Stop a minute to understand what you have. The rectangle has two sides of four stitches each. They will continue to have four stitches during the tip

shaping and will make a band around the edge of the mitten. The sides with three stitches will increase to the width of the mitten and will become the front (palm) and the back of the hand.

You will henceforth be knitting around, one needle at a time, turning your work clockwise. Just concentrate on the needle you are knitting as though the others weren't there. Soon your hands will find a way of holding the work so that the extra needles don't get in the way of the one you're knitting. Working four needles makes one round.

Back to work: Mark the corner where your yarn is for the beginning of the round. A small safety pin or a piece of contrasting yarn run through a stitch works well. Knit one round. **First increase round**: Pick up and knit one stitch at X (Fig 10). Knit three stitches. Pick up and knit one stitch at Y— two stitches increased. Knit across

Beginning rectangle on four needles.

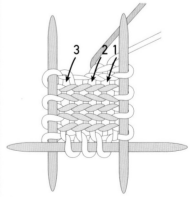

8. Rotate and knit across four stitches of next needle with ball yarn.

9. Pick up and knit three stitches along other edge. Then, following text, work across next needle (band), mark beginning of round, and work one round (four needles) on 14 stitches.

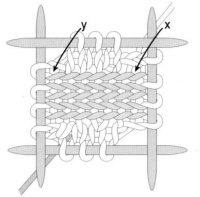

10. Increase round: pick up and knit one stitch at X, k3, pick up and knit one stitch at Y—five stitches on needle; knit four band stitches . . .

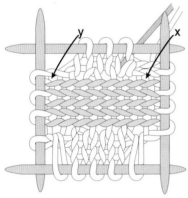

11. . . . pick up and knit one stitch at X, k3, pick up and knit one stitch at Y—five stitches; knit four band stitches—18 stitches around.

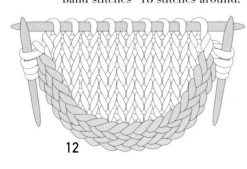

12

four band stitches with free needle. Pick up and knit one stitch at X as before (Fig. 11), knit three stitches, pick up and knit one stitch at Y—two stitches increased. Knit across four band stitches with free needle—a total of four stitches have been increased.

Knit one round even, then repeat the increase round. This time there will be five stitches between those you add. Continue to increase every other round.

When there are nine stitches on front and back needle, the tip will look like Fig 12. Continue increasing every other round until there are 21 sts on front and back needles.

On the next round, k2tog at the beginning of each 4-stitch band needle—three stitches remain.

You may now rearrange the stitches on the needles if you like. Knit the three band stitches and half the front stitches (10) on one needle, the other half of the front stitches (11) on the 2nd needle, the three band stitches and half the back on the 3rd needle, and the remaining stitches (the other half of the back) on the 4th needle. Knit around for five or six rounds.

It's now time to put in a pattern.

Two-color knitting

When you are going to knit a pattern, you follow a chart. I am going to give a detailed explanation of how a chart works.

Every square on the chart represents one stitch. The white squares represent the background color (MC, for main color). The shaded squares represent the pattern color (CC, for contrasting color). Each row of squares is one row of knitting. The chart represents the pattern as you will see it after it is knit. To reproduce it, you must follow the chart from right to left. This does not matter when the pattern is symmetrical, but can make a difference when it is not. Start at the bottom of the chart with row 1 and work up. All the mitten charts in this book show one-half of the mitten. For

4-stitch band decreased to 3 stitches.

Stitches rearranged.

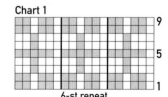

Chart 1

6-st repeat

one round, the chart is worked from right to left twice. The cuff charts usually show only one pattern repeat. To work these, you work from right to left, repeating the chart around the cuff.

Two-color, two-hand knitting, wrong side.

For the most part, patterns are composed of a number of stitches that are repeated around. In Chart 1, the repeat number is six. The heavy vertical lines on the chart indicate where you begin the pattern and show the stitches that are repeated. Thus the first round of this pattern will be knit: 1 stitch MC, 2 stitches CC.

The color you are not working with will be carried along the back of the piece until you use it again. Do not carry it too tightly. It helps to pull the stitches on the right-hand needle back on the needle every time you change color. As you pick up speed, this stretching of the stitches becomes part of your rhythm and you scarcely realize you're doing it. But the result is that the stitches are never pulled too tightly.

Two-color, two-hand knitting, right side.

Many people work with two colors by picking up one yarn, knitting the required number of stitches, dropping that yarn, and picking up the other one. There are times when this is a perfectly appropriate thing to do. But for smooth and speedy knitting without tangled yarns, learn to knit with both hands, that is, two-handed knitting.

If you normally hold your yarn with your right hand

Begin by knitting one stitch with MC. Drop that yarn and knit two stitches with CC. Knit one MC. Now, holding your knitting in your left hand, place the CC strand over your left index finger (point the finger). Then weave the strand under your middle finger and over the last two fingers. (This is the way I hold it. You may have to try different ways to lay the yarn to find something comfortable.) With your right hand, place the point of the right-hand needle into the next stitch. With that point hook the CC yarn that you're holding in your left hand and pull it through the stitch. Drop the stitch off the left-hand needle and you've made a stitch with your left hand. Make another CC stitch in the left-handed manner.

Pull stitches to avoid tight carries.

Continue making one stitch MC right-handed, two stitches CC left-handed, and work around all four needles, keeping CC positioned in your left hand and picking up MC with right hand. By the time you get around, the left-handed stitching will feel a little less awkward. By the time you finish the whole pattern, you may feel right at home with two-handed knitting.

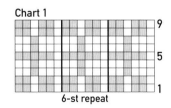

Chart 1

9

5

1

6-st repeat

If you normally hold your yarn with your left hand

Begin by knitting one stitch with MC. Add CC yarn and knit two stitches with CC. Now drop the CC yarn from your left hand. Knit one MC. With your right hand in its normal position, bring the CC yarn over your right index finger and under the other fingers, holding it with your little finger. (This is the way I hold it. You may find some other way to hold it comfortably in your right hand.) Place the point of the right-hand needle into the next stitch. With your right hand, wrap the CC yarn behind the point and then forward. With the point, pull the yarn through the stitch and drop the stitch off the left-hand needle. One right-handed stitch made. Make another CC stitch in the right-handed manner.

Work around all four needles making one MC stitch left-handed and two CC stitches right-handed. By the time you get around the right-handed knitting will be easy, though probably a good deal slower than left-handed knitting.

Looking at the chart, you will see that the next pattern row is the same as the first. So work around again. The 3rd row of the pattern is different. Between the vertical repeat lines on the chart, you see three MC, one CC, two MC. If you repeat that, the pattern comes out correct. But you will also see, looking beyond the vertical lines, that after the first CC there are five MC then one CC. So do the three MC and then start thinking one CC, five MC around. If you simplify the pattern repeats in your head each time you start a round, you will be able to finish the round without looking back to the chart.

Keeping your eyes on your knitting instead of on the chart also helps avoid mistakes. In this row, for example, if you see that you are working a CC st over a CC st on the previous round, you

Try on mitten to check for thumb placement.

will know that you've gone wrong. This is where charts are so much easier to use than directions written out in words and numbers. You can see, row by row, how a pattern is supposed to look.

So work through the nine rounds of this pattern, practicing two-handed knitting. When you finish, you will probably be almost to the thumb. (Put your hand in the mitten to see where the thumb should fit.) If you're not there yet, relax and knit around until you get there.

The thumb

When you reach the place where the thumb should join, place all the mitten stitches on hold and lay the mitten aside. Take the needles and begin the thumb by wrapping two needles in a figure-8 pattern just as you did at the tip of the mitten. This time wrap only three loops on each needle. Make a rectangle just as you did before and pick up three sts on each side as before—

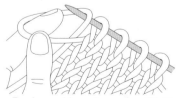

Backward loop increase (BL1): Make a backward loop on right-hand needle.

tubular bind-off

Leave a long end of yarn and thread it in a blunt needle. Assuming the first stitch on left needle is a knit stitch, bring yarn through first stitch as if to purl, leave st on needle.

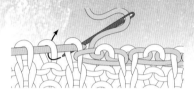

1. Take needle behind knit stitch, between first two stitches, and through purl stitch as if to knit. Leave stitches on needle.

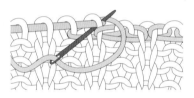

2. Bring yarn to front, then through knit stitch as if to knit and slip stitch off needle.

3. Take needle in front of purl stitch and through knit stitch as if to purl. Leave stitches on needle.

4. Bring yarn through purl stitch as if to purl and slip off needle.

5. Adjust tension. Repeat Steps 1-4.

12 stitches on four needles in a square. On the next round increase to 20 stitches as follows: * K2, [BL1, k1] 4 times; repeat from*. Now knit around until the thumb is long enough (try it on).

Insert the thumb in the mitten

Rearrange the thumb stitches onto two needles, ten stitches on each needle. Lay the mitten flat. Beginning with the 3rd stitch in from the side of the mitten, pick up ten stitches from the holding thread with one of your needles. (Don't worry about the holding thread. It can stay where it is. It all gets pulled out later.) Place the thumb on top of the mitten so that the three sets of ten stitches, each on its own needle, are lined up. With a separate piece of working yarn and another needle, use 3-needle bind-off to join the mitten stitches and the middle needle of thumb stitches. To do this, hold the two needles together in your left hand. Insert another needle in the first stitch

of the front needle, then the first stitch of the back needle. Knit these two stitches together. *Knit the next stitch on both needles together in the same way. There are now two stitches on the right-hand needle; pass the first over the 2nd. Repeat from* until there remains only one stitch on the right-hand needle, none on the left. Pull the end of the yarn through this stitch.

Now replace the mitten stitches on four needles using the other 10 thumb stitches in place of those bound off. Knit a few rounds. Then pull out the holding thread.

When you come to inserting the thumb on the second mitten, place it on the other side. That is, when your mitten is lying flat, palm up, one thumb will go on the right side, the other thumb on the left side.

Knit around until you come to your wrist.

Repeat the pattern from the chart in the same or a different color.

Use 3-needle bind-off to join mitten and thumb.

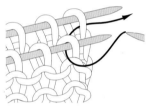

3-needle bind-off: K2tog (thumb stitch and mitten stitch) twice, bind first stitch off over second stitch.

Replace the bound-off mitten stitches with thumb stitches.

To finish the mitten, work four rounds of rib as follows: *K1b (knit one through the back of the stitch, thereby twisting the stitch), p1; repeat from* around. Bind off using tubular bind-off (or bind off in rib, if tubular bind-off seems to be too much trouble).

Other than weaving in the ends, the only finishing necessary will be closing up the spaces on each side of the thumb. (Those holes will be there whether you make mittens from the top down or the bottom up.) Turn the mitten inside out. With the ends left from binding off the thumb and mitten stitches together, close up the spaces by running the yarn under the purl bumps around the hole and pulling the yarn tight. Finish off the ends.

If you make this whole pair of mittens, you will be adept enough at all mitten techniques to move on to any of the mittens in this book (though you might want to avoid those I've noted as the hardest). Enjoy!

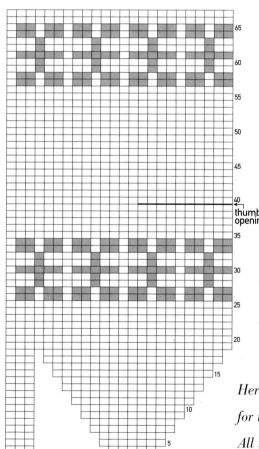

Here is a whole mitten chart for the beginner's mitten. All the patterns in this book are charted this way.

These are the general directions for making all the mittens in the book.

The mittens are worked from finger tip to wrist.

Materials

50g each of colors **A** and **B** will make a pair of mittens with large cuffs. Quantities for additional colors are included in the individual pattern. When you are using leftovers, count on 1 yard of each color for each round. That will be plenty.

Set of 5 double pointed needles (dpn) in the size needed to get the gauge (4–7), preferably short (5").

Optional: 11½" circular needle or a set of 7" dpns. Set of dpn 2 sizes smaller for wrist.

Gauge

For average adult woman's mitten, 6½ stitches equal 1". Mittens are shown in this size and were knit at this gauge.

FOR INVISIBLE-THUMB MITTENS WITH PLAIN BANDS

1 begin the plain band

1 Figure-8 cast-on
Shaded yarn is the tail yarn, unshaded yarn is the ball yarn. Hold two short (5") dpn together, one on top of the other. Leaving a 5" tail, wrap **B** yarn in a figure-8 around the needles until there are 4 loops on each needle.

2 With a third dpn, knit loops off top needle.

3 Turn the work (keeping tail where it is) and purl back.

4 Turn the work and rotate the needles so the unknit loops are at the top and the tail is on your right. The top loops are loose. Tighten them by using a third dpn, pulling stitch by stitch from left to right.

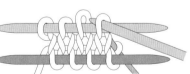

5 With the tail yarn, knit into the back loops of these 4 stitches.

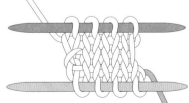

6 Rotate the needles so first dpn is on top and the tail yarn is on your right. Knit across the 4 stitches with ball yarn.

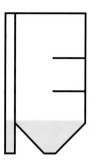

2 shape the mitten tip

Now you need to refer to the mitten chart. You might want to photocopy the chart or just copy the beginning of the chart for reference as you work this section. Our example is mitten chart 4-3 from p. 41.

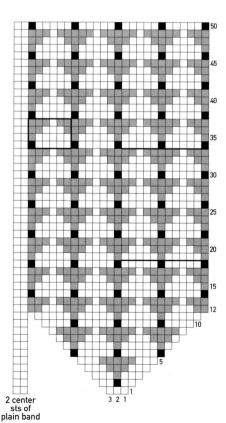

2 center sts of plain band

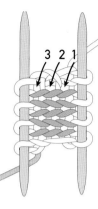

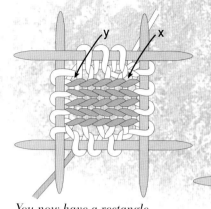

7 With a third dpn and following colors on chart row 1, pick up and knit 3 stitches along edge.

The 2½ stitches shaded here will be seen as the band on the tip of the mitten.

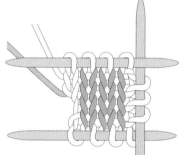

8 Rotate and with a fourth dpn, following band color, knit across 4 stitches of next needle.

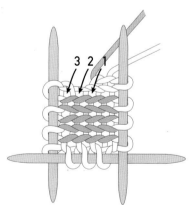

9 Repeat steps 7 and 8, following colors of chart row 1 and knitting 4 band stitches—14 stitches in round (see illustration at top of next column).

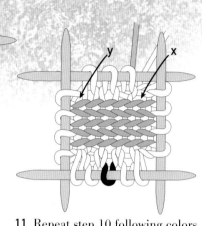

You now have a rectangle. The four stitches at each end form "the band." The 3 stitches at the top and bottom will become the back and palm of the mitten.

10 Work chart row 2 (first increase round): Following colors on chart, pick up and knit 1 stitch at X, knit 3 stitches from dpn, then pick up and knit 1 stitch at Y—5 stitches on needle. Knit 4 band stitches from next dpn. Note the color change at the center stitch (see illustration for step 11).

11 Repeat step 10 following colors on chart row 2 and knitting 4 band stitches—18 stitches in round.

Following the chart for colors and increases, continue to pick up and knit one stitch at each end of palm and back on every round (chart rows 3–12 in our example—58 stitches in round). When all stitches have been increased, decrease the band to 2 stitches by working k2tog, ssk across each set of 4 band stitches (chart row 13–54 stitches in round). At this point you may change to longer dpn, rearranging the stitches or not as you prefer. After a few more rounds, you may change to a 12" circular needle.

3 work the mitten to thumb opening

There are 2 heavy lines on the chart, each across 12 stitches. Continue to knit from the chart until you reach the top 12-stitch line. This is the thumb opening (on p. 27 the thumb opening is on top of chart row 33). Put the 12 thumb stitches on hold and lay the mitten aside. (If you have a circular needle or 2 sets of dpns or if you have already made the thumb, there is no need to put stitches on a holding thread. But having the stitches on an extra piece of thread means fewer needles to manipulate as you insert the thumb.)

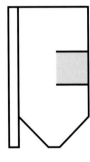

4 work the thumb

Working Steps 1-9, begin the thumb the same way as for the plain band mitten, but on step 1, figure-8 wrap **only 3 loops** on each dpn. (There will be no band on the thumb.) Knit 1 round on 12 stitches. On next round, work [k1, M1] 3 times on each dpn—6 stitches on each dpn. The thumb chart begins at the first row that has 12 stitches underlined. **For small-patterned mittens**: work the 12 stitches of this row twice for the first pattern round of the thumb. **For large-patterned mittens**: Work each row of the thumb section of the chart from right to left over 12 stitches, then from left to right over the remaining 12 stitches.

For all mittens: Work around in pattern to the top 12-stitch line.

insert the invisible thumb in the left mitten

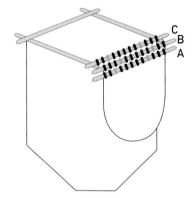

12 thumb stitches on needle A exactly match mitten stitches on needle C. Using 3-needle bind-off, bind off the stitches on needles B and C together. Replace the bound-off mitten stitches with remaining thumb stitches from needle A.

5 insert the invisible thumb

For the left mitten: 1 Put the thumb stitches on 2 dpn so that the stitches on 1 dpn match exactly the **first** 12 mitten stitches inside the band (the other needle's stitches may or may not match).

2 Put the matching mitten stitches (those first 12 stitches inside the band) on a dpn.

3 Now lay the thumb on the mitten as shown in illustration above right.

4 With ground color and another dpn, work a 3-needle bind-off across stitches on needles B and C leaving a tail of yarn at each end to close up the space remaining when the mitten is finished.

5 Now replace the bound-off mitten stitches with the remaining thumb stitches and work to the top of the mitten chart (Row 50 of chart on p. 27). **Note**: If you want to you can put half the thumb and mitten stitches on a holding thread and join them when the mitten is finished, either with a 3-needle bind-off or by grafting.

    For right mitten: Work as for left mitten but match the thumb stitches to the **last** 12 stitches of the palm. The only difference between the right and left mitten is this placement of the thumb.

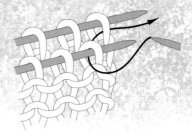

3-needle bind-off

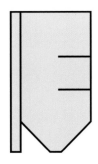

6 shape the wrist

After working last row of chart, knit 1 round in the same color as the first round of the cuff, decreasing evenly to 44 stitches. Follow directions for the desired cuff. If you want to finish the mitten without a cuff, work 2½" in k1b, p1 rib on 44 stitches.

Place right sides together, back stitches on one needle and front stitches on another. *K2tog (one from front needle and one from back needle). Rep from* once. Bind first stitch off over 2nd stitch. Continue to k2tog (one front stitch and one back stitch) and bind off across.

a clarification

How plain is a plain band? As you will notice on several of the mitten charts, there may be color changes on a "plain" band. These are made because the pattern color or the ground color changes on these rounds. What a plain band does not have is a vertical stripe. Bands with vertical stripes are called striped bands and begin a little differently as you will see on the next page.

FOR INVISIBLE-THUMB MITTENS WITH STRIPED BANDS

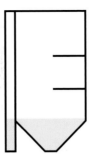

1 begin the striped band

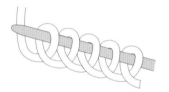

1 Cast on 5 stitches with **A** by the backward loop method.

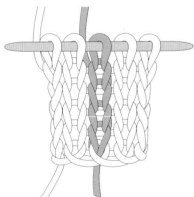

2 Knit across 2 stitches **A**, 1 stitch **B** (leave a 3" tail of **B**), 2 stitches **A**. Work 4 more rows in stockinette stitch maintaining the stripe as established (at color changes, bring new color under old).

You now have a small rectangle with a stripe down the center.

2 shape the mitten tip

Now you need to refer to the mitten chart. You might want to photocopy the chart or just copy the beginning of the chart for reference as you work through this section. Our example is mitten chart 4-14 from p. 63.

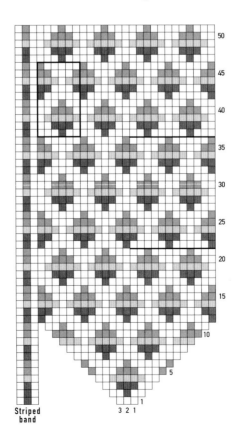

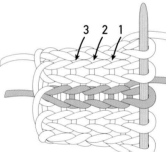

3 Begin to knit around: with a second dpn, pick up and knit 3 stitches on the side of the rectangle…

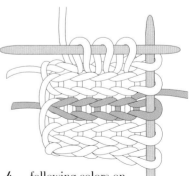

4 …following colors on chart row 1.

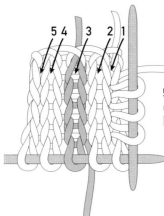

5 4   3   2 1

5 With another dpn, knit up stitches along the bottom of the rectangle…

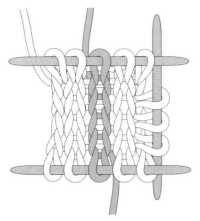

6 …2A, 1B, 2A. (If color **B** isn't used in Step 4, use the tail of the **B** cast-on to knit the **B** stitch.) In knitting up these stitches, insert your needle right into the stitch of the first row so that the knit-up is virtually invisible.

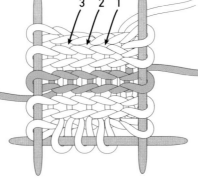

3   2   1

7 With a fourth dpn and following colors on chart, pick up and knit 3 stitches on the side; knit 5 band stitches—16 stitches in round.

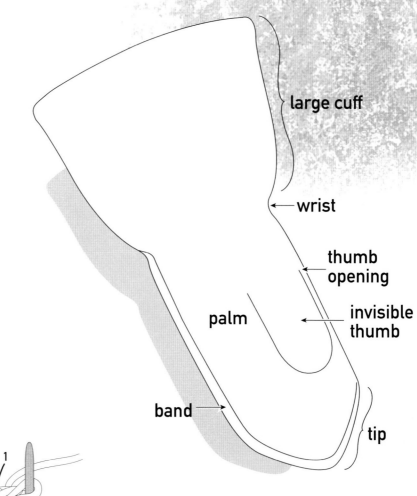

large cuff

wrist

thumb opening

palm

invisible thumb

band

tip

Follow General Directions for Invisible-Thumb Mitten with Plain Band beginning with Step 10 (p. 27), working 5 band stitches instead of 4. When all stitches have been increased, decrease the band to 3 stitches by k2tog, k1, ssk.

FOR SORE-THUMB MITTENS

Follow General Directions for Invisible-Thumb Mittens through shaping the mitten tip. For 2-stitch bands, use Plain Band beginning (p. 26). For more than 2 stitches use Striped Band beginning (p. 30) with number of stitches called for in pattern.

Our example mitten chart is

6-1 from p. 105.

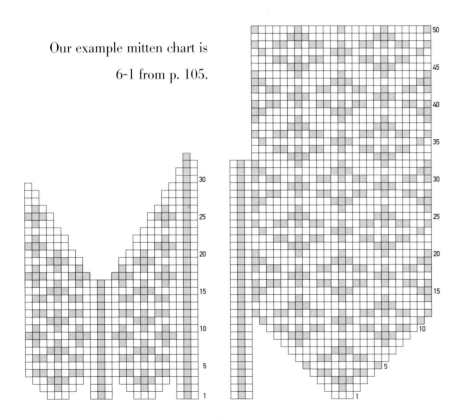

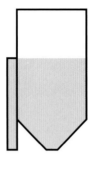

3 work the mitten to sore-thumb opening

Continue to knit from the chart until you reach the thumb. This place is indicated on the chart by the abrupt ending of the band (after row 32 on our example chart). To custom fit the mitten, try it on and stop where it is comfortable. Mark the row at which you stopped on the chart.

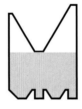

4 work the sore thumb

Begin the thumb the same way you began the tip of the mitten and follow the thumb chart. Exceptions occur if the band goes over the top of the hand from back to palm and are explained in the individual instructions. When you come to the place on the thumb chart where the center band stitches disappear (after row 16 on our example), it is time to insert the thumb.

5 insert the sore thumb

Arrange the thumb so that its center band stitches are on one needle. Line up these stitches with the matching mitten band stitches. Place right sides together and bind them off together using a 3-needle bind-off (p. 29). (Or put all these stitches on hold and work them together when the mitten is done.)

Mitten 6-3 with a sore thumb
(on the left) and an invisible
thumb (on the right).

Now you have to work around the thumb stitches and the hand stitches following the pattern for both. I find it easiest to keep thumb stitches on 2 or 3 needles for a couple of rounds before putting them all on an 11" circular needle or 4 dpn.

On the second round you must start decreasing the thumb stitches. To do this, knit together the last thumb stitch and the first mitten stitch as you go around, and ssk the last mitten stitch and the first thumb stitch of the round. Continue decreasing in the same manner, following the charts, until you reach the wrist.

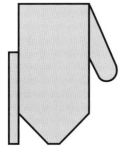

6 Shape the wrist

After working last row of chart, knit 1 round in color of first round of cuff, decreasing evenly to 44 stitches. Follow directions for the desired cuff. If you want to finish the mitten without a cuff, work 2½" in k1b, p1 rib on 44 stitches.

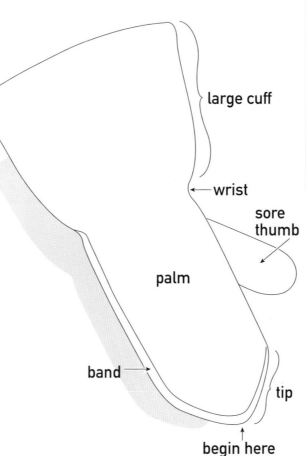

large cuff

← wrist

sore thumb

palm

band →

tip

↑ begin here

4 | small-patterned mittens

The mittens in this chapter have patterns with a 4, 6, 8 or 12-stitch repeat. On the charts, the outlined box shows one complete pattern repeat. Some are extremely simple, some not quite so, but all tend to be less demanding than larger patterns. They are also more flexible. That is, they invite various color choices, changes in pattern or background color within the mitten, and embellishments.

The primary advantage of these patterns over all the large-patterned mittens comes in working the invisible thumb. On these mittens, the thumb takes 24 stitches so each of these patterns can be worked continuously around. If the pattern is larger than 12 stitches, the thumb must be worked with a front pattern and a back pattern.

If you change the size of these mittens more than is possible by just changing yarn and gauge, you may destroy this thumb advantage. It depends on how many stitches you change. For instance, on a 42-stitch mitten you probably want an 18-stitch thumb. A 6-stitch pattern will work evenly here but a 4, 8, or 12 won't.

Since the thumb is worked separately, you may want to knit it first if you are following my placement. If you are going to fit it on your hand, you might want to cut off about ten yards of each color before you start the mitten. Then you won't have to cut the working yarn when you get to the thumb.

All the small-patterned mittens follow the general directions in Chapter 3 for materials and methods. Begin the mitten with plain (p. 26) or striped (p. 30) band. This is indicated at the top of each set of instructions. For any unfamiliar techniques or abbreviations, see Chapter 9, p. 132. See Chapter 7, p. 126 for edge finishes and Chapter 8, p. 130 for adding a warm and voluptuous lining.

Feel free to vary embellishments, edgings, and colors, not to mention using nubbly or rainbow-dyed yarn. Furthermore, all the mittens in this chapter are decreased to 44 stitches at the wrist, so any of the cuffs can be knit onto any of the mittens.

With a four-stitch repeat and only two different rows that alternate, this is the easiest pattern to work. By the same token, it is also a bit boring. One thing to look out for: you must be consistent with which color you hold in which hand. The slightest differences in tension will show up in a pattern this simple. To keep track of what you're doing when you put your knitting down, put a slip knot in the yarn you hold in your right hand. Pull it out when you begin to knit again.

MITTEN

Follow General Directions for Mitten with Plain Band and work to top of Mitten chart.

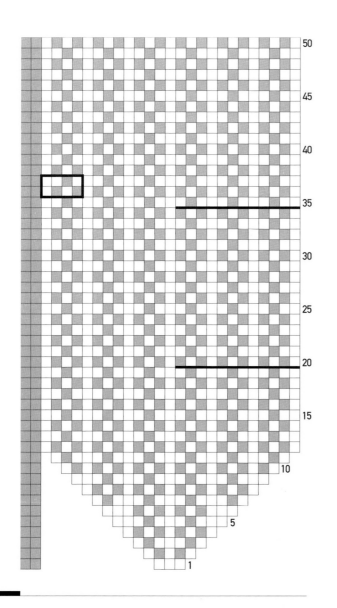

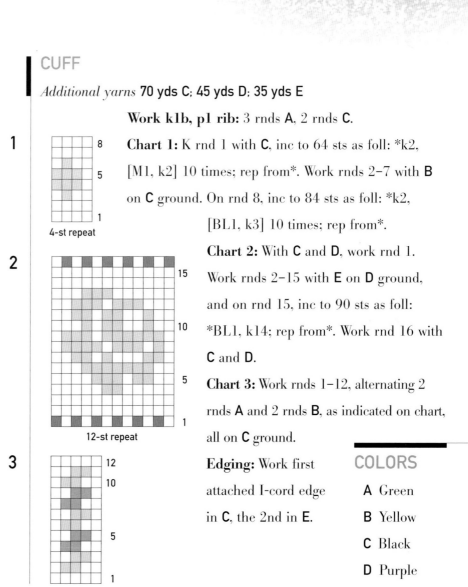

CUFF

Additional yarns **70 yds C; 45 yds D; 35 yds E**

Work k1b, p1 rib: 3 rnds **A**, 2 rnds **C**.

Chart 1: K rnd 1 with **C**, inc to 64 sts as foll: *k2, [M1, k2] 10 times; rep from*. Work rnds 2–7 with **B** on **C** ground. On rnd 8, inc to 84 sts as foll: *k2, [BL1, k3] 10 times; rep from*.

Chart 2: With **C** and **D**, work rnd 1. Work rnds 2–15 with **E** on **D** ground, and on rnd 15, inc to 90 sts as foll: *BL1, k14; rep from*. Work rnd 16 with **C** and **D**.

Chart 3: Work rnds 1–12, alternating 2 rnds **A** and 2 rnds **B**, as indicated on chart, all on **C** ground.

Edging: Work first attached I-cord edge in **C**, the 2nd in **E**.

COLORS

A Green

B Yellow

C Black

D Purple

E Red

Much of the clarity and simplicity of this pattern is blurred by its being worked in colors with little contrast. The swatch below shows the difference in effect when contrasting colors are used. It is also easier to work. Since this is a 12-stitch repeat, there are only two pattern repeats on the thumb. With six stitches (half a repeat) on each thumb needle, it is a bit harder to work than other small-pattern repeats.

MITTEN

Follow General Directions for Mitten with Plain Band and work to top of Mitten chart.

Before beginning to knit, thread 18 small (3mm) silver beads on **A**. Work these beads into the back of the mitten only (not the palm) where indicated on the chart.

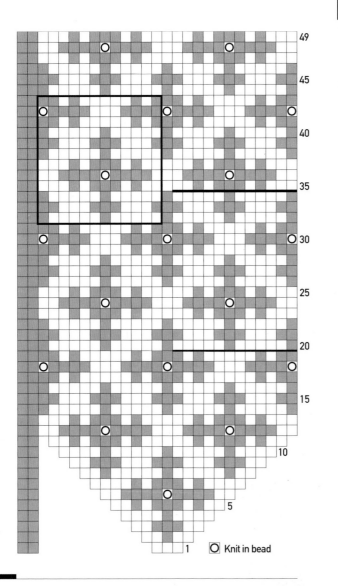

O Knit in bead

CUFF

Additional materials **50g C; 70 yds D; 15 yds E; 92 small (3mm) silver beads (used for back of hand and cuff)**

Work k1b, p1 rib: 3 rnds **A**, 2 rnds **D**, 3 rnds **B**.

Change to **C**. K next rnd, inc to 84 sts as foll: *k2, [BL1, k1] 20 times; rep from*.

K 2 rnds **C**, 1 rnd **D**, 1 rnd **B**, 1 rnd **D**.

Chart: Work 23 rnds of left or right cuff chart (depending on mitten) with **D** on **C** ground.

K 1 rnd **D**, 1 rnd **B**, 1 rnd **D**, 3 rnds **C**.

Edging: With **A**, k 1 rnd, p 1 rnd. String 28 beads on **B**. With **B**, k 1 rnd, knitting a bead into every third st. With **A**, k 1 rnd, then p 1 rnd. With **D**, k 1 rnd, p 1 rnd. Bind off purlwise with **D**.

Embellish: Using photo as guide, work Smyrna Cross st in **E** in center of boxes on cuffs.

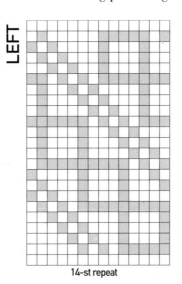

LEFT

14-st repeat

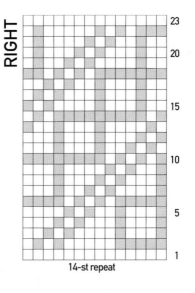

RIGHT

14-st repeat

COLORS

A Dark green

B Blue

C White

D Purple

E Pink

A very simple 6-stitch pattern, effective in two, three, or four colors. It can also be done with scrap yarns, changing colors at every pattern repeat. To see if you have enough of any one scrap to do a pattern repeat, estimate about one yard per round for pattern knitting.

MITTEN

Follow General Directions for Mitten with Plain Band and work to top of mitten chart.

Dotted lines on the chart indicate that the ground color alternates from **B** to **C**; this color

change also produces a two-color "plain" band.

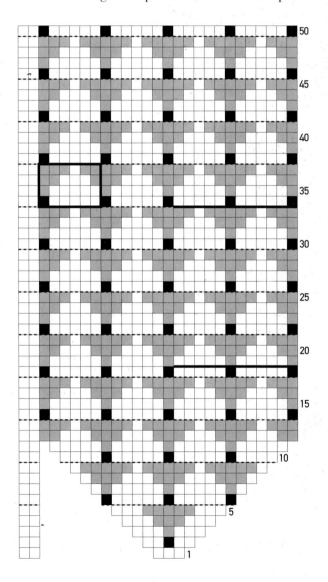

CUFF

Additional yarns **25 yds C and 45 yds D (used in mitten as well as cuff); 40 yds E**

Wrist pat: Rnds 1–2 With **E**, k 1 rnd, p 1 rnd. **Rnd 3** With **B**, *k1, sl 1 with

yarn in back (wyib); rep from*. **Rnd 4** With **B**, *p1, sl 1 around wyib; rep

from*. **Rnds 5–8** Rep rnds 1-4. With **E**, k 1 rnd, p 1 rnd.

Change to **A**. K next rnd, inc to 80 sts as foll: *K4, [BL1, k1] 18 times;

rep from*.

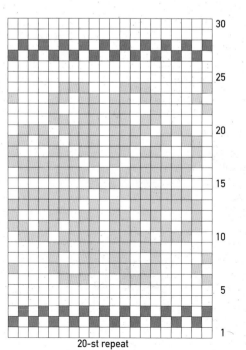

20-st repeat

Chart: Work 30 rows of cuff chart

using **D** on rnds 2-3 and 27–28,

B on rnds 6-24, all on **A** ground.

Edging: Work rnds 1–8 of wrist

pat with **C** instead of **B**. With **C**,

work fringe edge.

COLORS

A Dark green

B Pink

C Purple

D Light green

E Orange

This 12-stitch, 12-row pattern is less complicated than it looks. Four of the 12 rows (1, 5, 7, 11) are a 1-2 alternation of colors; four others are almost as simple. The four remaining rows (2, 4, 8, 10), all the same, alternate colors as follows: *1-2, 1-1, 1-2, 1-3; repeat from*. It's a row that's fun to work, though it does take some attention. I find the thumb a little hard to keep track of. I'm not at all sure why.

Since the ground color has many fewer stitches than the pattern color, the ground keeps trying to read as pattern. This is true even here, where I've made the pattern bright red, a warm color that is alleged to come forward.

MITTEN

Follow General Directions for Mitten with Striped Band and work to top of Mitten chart.

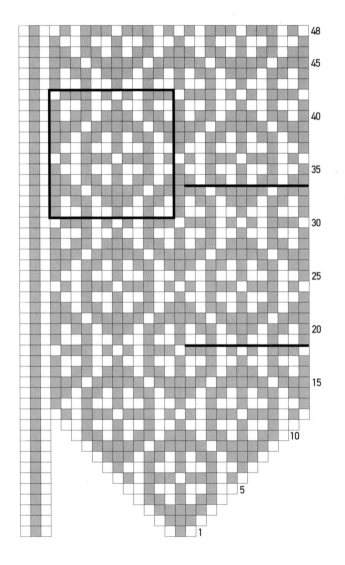

48
45
40
35
30
25
20
15
10
5
1

CUFF

Additional yarns **50g C**; **24 yds D**

Work k1b, p1 rib: 3 rnds **A**, 2 rnds **B**, 3 rnds **C**.

With **C**, k 1 rnd, inc to 65 sts as foll: K2, [M1, k2] 21 times.

Chart 1: Work rnds 1–5 with **D** on **C** ground. On rnd 6, inc to 80 sts as foll: K5, [BL1, k4] 15 times.

Chart 2: Work 23 rnds of chart using **B** on rnds 1 and 23 and **A** and **B** on rnds 2 and 22. On rnds 3–21, use **A** on **C** ground.

Chart 1: Repeat chart 1, omitting increases on rnd 6.

Edging: Work double roll edge as foll: With **C**, k 1 rnd, p 3 rnds. With **B**, k 2 rnds, p 3 rnds. With **B** bind off purlwise.

1

5

1

5-st repeat

2

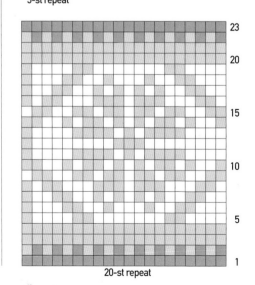

23
20
15
10
5
1

20-st repeat

COLORS

A Purple

B Red

C Blue green

D Yellow

This is not an easy pattern to work—at least I do not find it so. Once it's under way it is rather fun because it consists of a run of four different rows that then reverse. Still, it's easy to get confused.

Since this is an 8-stitch pattern, the thumb consists of three pattern repeats. This gives it the cheerful characteristic of matching the mitten whether it is pointing up toward the tip or flopping down toward the wrist. (Not everyone cares about such details, but some of us cherish them.)

MITTEN

Follow General Directions for Mitten with Striped Band and
work to top of Mitten chart.

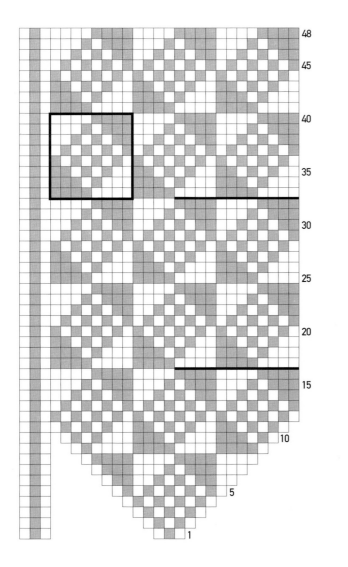

CUFF

Additional materials **50g each of A and B; 172 small (3mm) silver beads**

Wrist pat: With **A**, [p 1 rnd, k 1 rnd] twice, inc on last rnd to 66 sts as foll:
K2, M1; rep from. String 86 beads on **B**.

Chart 1: Work 11 rnds in chart pat with **B** on **A** ground and knit in beads
where indicated on rnds 1 and 11.

With **A**, k 2 rnds, inc in 2nd rnd to 90 sts as foll: *K3, [BL1, k3, BL1, k2]
6 times; rep from*.

With **B**, [k 1 rnd, p 1 rnd] twice.

Chart 2: Work 16 rnds in chart pat with **B** on **A** ground. On
rnd 17, k, inc to 102 sts as foll: *BL1, k7, BL1, k8; rep from*.
*With **A**, k 1 rnd, p 1 rnd. Rep from* with **B**.

With **A**, k 1 rnd, knitting in a bead in every 3rd st.

With **A**, *p2, k1b; rep from*.

With **B**, k 1 rnd, p 1 rnd.

Edging: With **A**, work fringe edge.

Embellish: Using photo as guide, work stem
st with **A** and **B** between garter st ridges.

1

6-st repeat

2

15-st repeat

○ Knit in bead

COLORS

A Black

B White

The violet dots on these mittens have been added afterwards with duplicate stitch. If you wear the mitten on one hand while you sew with the other, you don't risk sewing back and palm together. If you prefer, it isn't too clumsy to knit it in as you go: every fifth round will have three colors with a 7-stitch carry. The thumb, however, is hard because this carry won't easily lie flat and you have to catch two colors. You might want to duplicate stitch only the thumb. You can also just leave out the fourth color— the mitten looks fine with green dots instead of violet.

Although I used a 2-stitch band, the 3-stitch band is charted here. It gets rid of long carries at the tip of the mitten.

MITTEN

Follow General Directions for Mitten with Striped Band and
work to top of Mitten chart.

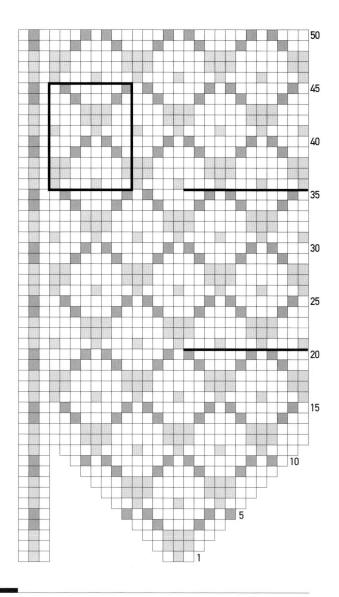

CUFF

Additional yarns **45 yds C and 70 yds D (used in mitten and cuff)**

Work k1b, p1 rib: 3 rnds **B**, 2 rnds **C**, 3 rnds **B**.

Change to **A**. K 1 rnd, inc to 64 sts as foll: *K2, [BL1, k2] 10 times;
rep from*.

Chart 1: Work 5 rnds in chart pat with **D** on **A** ground. On rnd 6,
inc to 84 sts as foll: *K2, [BL1, k3] 10 times; rep from*.

Chart 2: Work 18 rnds in chart pat with **D** on **B** ground. On rnd
19, inc to 96 sts as foll: *K7, BL1;
rep from*.

With **A**, k 1 rnd.

Chart 1: Rep 6 rnds of Chart 1,
omitting increases on rnd 6.

Edging: With **D**, work fringe edge.

1

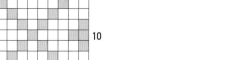

4-st repeat

2

12-st repeat

COLORS

A White

B Green

C Blue

D Violet

An extremely simple 6-stitch pattern that can look quilted or checkered depending on the colors (see swatch below). Colors of similar intensity give the slightly three-dimensional look.

The red on the cuff was worked in duplicate stitch. There isn't any real need for it; the mitten looked fine without it. But I was in a mood for lily-gilding.

MITTEN

Follow General Directions for Mitten with Plain Band and work to
top of Mitten chart. When shaping wrist, decrease to 40 stitches.

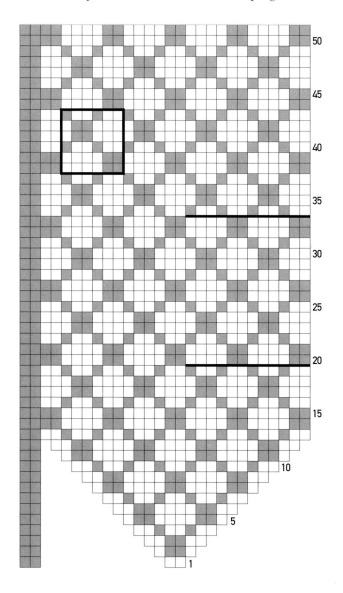

CUFF

Additional yarns **60 yds C; 50g D**

Work k1b, p1 rib: 6 rnds **B**.

Chart: Change to **D** and work 37 rnds of cuff chart with **C** on **D** ground.
On inc rnds 3, 5, 7, 9, etc., work lifted inc before and after single **C** st as
indicated on chart—8 incs per rnd.

Edging: With **B**, work
5 rnds k1b, p1 rib.
Work tubular bind-off.

Embellish: Work
duplicate st in **B** as
indicated on chart.

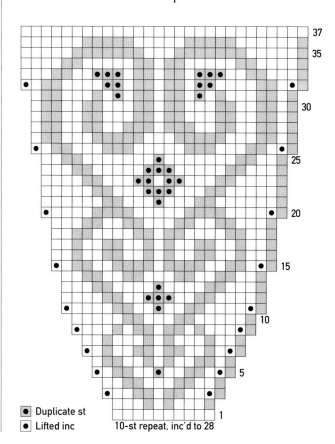

● Duplicate st
● Lifted inc

10-st repeat, inc'd to 28

COLORS

A Purple

B Red

C Green

D Violet

This is an easy, versatile pattern. You can vary the look dramatically by using different colors. Even though there are two pattern colors, it's a good choice for a first mitten project. On the other hand, the cuff I've paired it with demands a lot of attention. Much simpler ones would look wonderful.

MITTEN

Follow General Directions for Mittens with Plain Band and
work to top of Mitten chart.

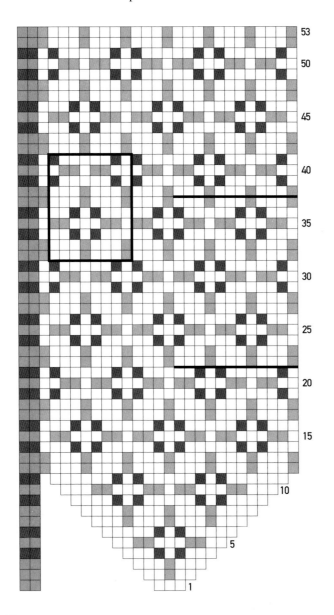

CUFF

Additional yarns **25 yds B; 50g C (used in mitten and cuff)**

Work k1b, p1 rib: 4 rnds in **A**. Change to **B**. K next rnd, inc to 64 sts as
foll: *K2, [BL1, k2] 10 times; rep from*.

Chart: Work 37 rnds of
cuff chart with **C** on **B**
ground. On inc rnds 5, 9,
13, and 17, work backward
loop inc (BL1) as indicated
on chart—8 incs per rnd.

Edging: With **A**, work 5
rnds in k1b, p1 rib. Work
tubular bind-off.

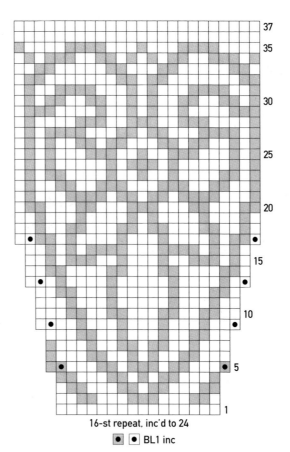

16-st repeat, inc'd to 24

◉ ◉ BL1 inc

COLORS

A Black

B Violet

C Orange

Despite its simplicity, I find this pattern a delight to do. It's a 6-stitch repeat with three different rows that follow the order: 1, 1, 1, 2, 3, 2. It would be especially good to make if you're practicing carrying both yarns in one hand.

If alternating groups of three rows were worked in different colors, it would look like a totally different pattern (see swatch below).

MITTEN

Follow General Directions for Mitten with Plain Band and
work to top of Mitten chart.

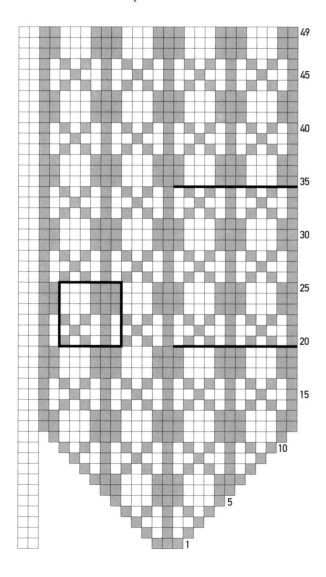

CUFF

Additional yarns **50g each of C and D**

Work k1b, p1 rib: 3 rnds with **B**.

With **A**, k 1 rnd, p 2 rnds. With **C**, k 1 rnd, then work 2 rnds k1b,
p1 rib. With **C**, k next rnd, inc to 64 sts as foll: *K2, [M1, k2) 10
times; rep from*.

Chart: Work 29 rnds of cuff chart with **D** on **C** ground. On inc rnds
9, 18, and 22, work lifted inc as
indicated on chart—8 incs per rnd.
Work heavy dotted lines on chart as
foll: After working rnd 15 or 29, with
A, k 1 rnd, p 2 rnds.

Edging: With **D**, work
fringe edge.

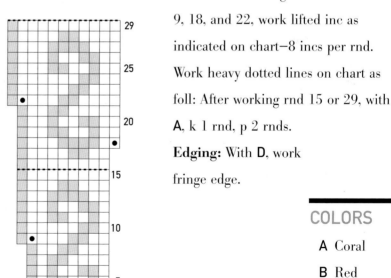

8-st repeat inc'd to 11

COLORS

A Coral

B Red

C Purple

D Green

This 4-stitch, 4-row repeat combines pleasing variety with utter simplicity. The asymmetry of the pattern makes the right and left thumbs different. You can work them the same, but care is necessary in arranging the stitches for insertion. Duplicate stitch adds the third color to the leaf pattern on the cuff.

MITTEN

Follow General Directions for Mitten with Plain Band
and work to top of Mitten chart. Work second mitten with
color **C** instead of **A**.

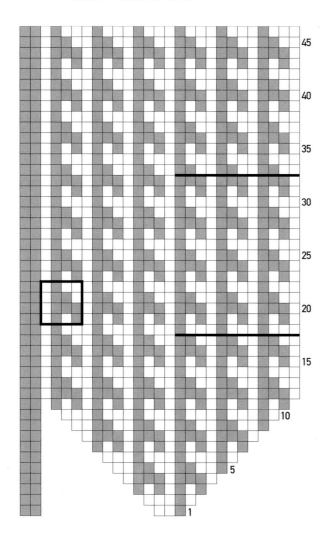

CUFF

Additional yarns **50g C** (used in mitten and cuff); **25 yds D**; **60 yds E**

Work k1b, p1 rib: 3 rnds **A**, 1 rnd **B**, 3 rnds **A**.

Chart 1: With **D**, k rnd 1, inc to 84 sts as foll: *K2, [BL1, k1] 20 times; rep from*. Work rnds 2–9 with **B** on **D** ground. Work rnds 10–12 with **A** on **C** ground.

Chart 2: With **D**, k rnd 1, inc to 90 sts as foll: *K14, BL1; rep from* 6 times. Work rnds 2–25 with **E** on **C** ground. Work rnds 26–27 with **A**.

Edging: With **B**, work 4 rnds k1b, p1 rib. Work tubular bind-off.

Embellish: Work duplicate st in leaves as indicated on chart 2.

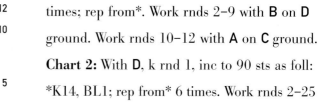

1

6-st repeat

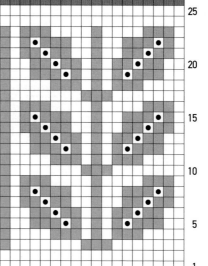

2

18-st repeat

● Duplicate st with D

COLORS

A Red

B Gold

C Purple

D Black

E Green

This is one
example of scrap mittens.
About 12 yards of each
color are needed for the
mittens, about 20 yards
total including the cuff.
The mitten itself is simple;
the cuff not so. There are
several very long carries.
But many cuff patterns
would go well with this
pattern, among them 4-7,
4-9, 4-13, 5-5, and 5-12.

MITTEN

Follow General Directions for Mitten with Plain Band and work to top of Mitten chart, using photo as guide for color changes.

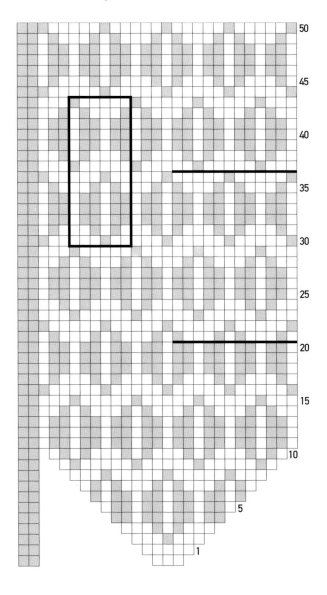

CUFF

Additional yarns **60 yds B; 50g C; assorted colors of scrap yarn**

Work k1b, p1 rib: 6 rnds **C**.

With **C**, k next rnd, inc to 64 sts as foll: *K2, [M1, k2] 10 times; rep from*.

Chart: Work 48 rnds of cuff chart using colors as desired or using photo as guide. On inc rnds 5, 6, 11, etc., work lifted inc or backward loop inc (BL1) before and after the single pattern color st as indicated on chart—8 incs per rnd.

Note: On rnds 17, 23, and 39 you can slip the first st of each rep and work with ground color only.

Edging: With **A** and **B**, work braid edge.

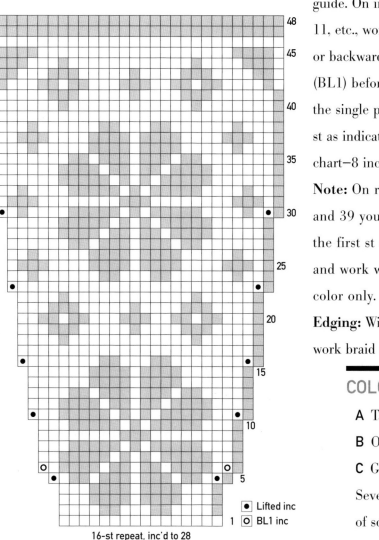

● Lifted inc
○ BL1 inc

16-st repeat, inc'd to 28

COLORS

A Tan

B Orange

C Green

Seven assorted colors of scrap yarn

*A most versatile
pattern. It looks totally
different in two contrasting
colors, different again in
similar colors—two, three,
or four. I find it an
enjoyable one to work—
simple, but with enough
variety to avoid boredom.*

MITTEN

Follow General Directions for Mitten with Striped Band and
work to top of Mitten chart.

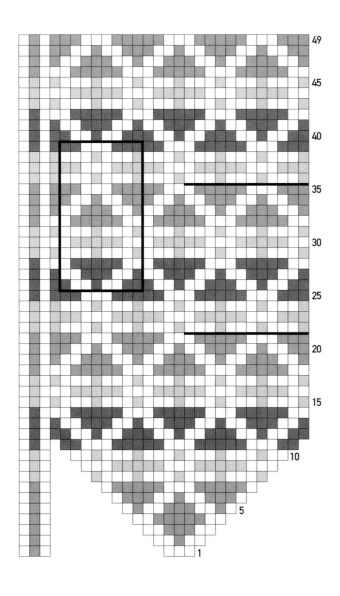

CUFF

Additional yarns **30 yds C**; **45 yds D (used in mitten as well as cuff)**

Work k1b, p1 rib: 3 rnds **A**, 2 rnds **D**, 3 rnds **A**.

With **A**, k 2 rnds, inc to 88 sts as foll: **Rnd 1** *K2, BL1; rep from*
around. **Rnd 2** *K3, BL1; rep from* around.

Work cuff pattern: Rnd 1 With **C**, *ssk (left dec), k3, BL1, k1,
BL1, k3, k2tog (right dec); rep from*. **Rnd 2** Knit. **Rnds 3–6** Rep
rnds 1–2 twice. **Rnd 7** With **A**, rep rnd 1. **Rnds 8, 10, 12** Purl.
Rnds 9, 11 Knit.

Rep rnds 1–12 twice, the first time with **D** and **A**, then with **B** and **A**.

Edging: With **A**, p 1 row, bind off and make bobbles as foll: *Bind
off 5 sts purlwise, make bobble in next st, bind off 6 sts purlwise
(the bobble plus 5 more sts); rep from* around.

To make bobble: K1-yo-k1-yo-k1 in one
st—5 sts. Turn. Sl 1, k4, turn. Sl 1, p4, turn.
Sl 1, k4. Pass the 2nd st, the 3rd, the 4th,
then the 5th st over first st and off the
needle. Turn. K 1.

COLORS

A Black

B Tan

C Green

D Orange

This mitten is a repeat of 4-9. I did it by mistake and couldn't decide which to leave out. The pattern and ground colors are reversed on the mittens. I like the effect and it keeps the project from becoming tedious— the one real disadvantage of having to make two.

Someone may notice in the picture that I made one cuff larger than the other. It was a mistake, pure and simple. The directions are given for the narrower cuff. If you want a fuller one, add 10 stitches at the beginning and continue.

MITTEN

Follow General Directions for Mitten with Plain Band and
work to top of Mitten chart, using photo as guide for colors
on mitten and cuff.

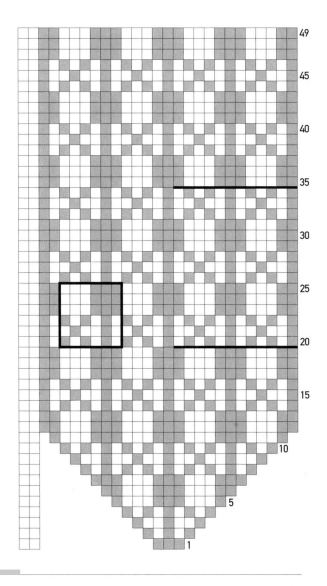

CUFF

Additional yarns **35 yds each of C and D**

Work garter st: K 1 rnd, then p 1 rnd with **B**. Rep last 2 rnds with
A, then **B**, then **A**, then **B**. With **A**, k 1 rnd, inc to 70 sts as foll:
K2, [BL1, k2] 7 times, [BL1, k1] 6 times; rep from.

Chart: Work 13 rnds in chart pat with **D** on **A** ground.

With **A**, k 2 rnds, inc to 90 sts on 1st rnd as foll: [K3, BL1, k4,
BL1] 10 times.

Work garter st: *K 1 rnd, then p 1 rnd with **B**; rep from* with **A**.
With **B**, k 2 rnds.

Chart: Work 13 rnds of chart with **C** on **B** ground.
With **B**, k 2 rnds.

Work garter st: *K 1 rnd, then p 1 rnd with **A**; rep from* with **B**.

Edging: With **D**, work fringe edge.

Embellish: Using photo as guide, work duplicate st in **C** in the
middle of squares on back of hand.

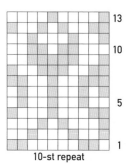

10-st repeat

COLORS

A Tan

B Green

C Blue green

D Purple

This is one of my favorite patterns, large or small. It does well in many color combinations or as a scrap mitten. Everything holds together if the color in the center of the motif stays the same throughout. (30 yards of yarn would be needed for all the centers.)

The Celtic pattern on the cuff (from Celtic Charted Designs by Co Spinhoven, published by Dover) is easier to knit than to draw, but that is not saying a whole lot. It takes careful row-by-row attention.

MITTEN

Follow General Directions for Mitten with Striped
Band and work to top of Mitten chart.

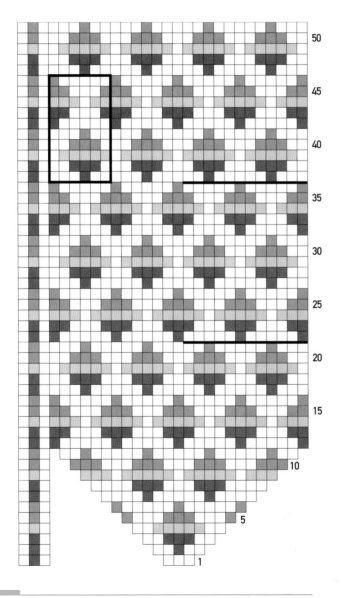

CUFF

Additional yarns **75 yds C and 35 yds D** (used in mitten as well as cuff); **50g E**

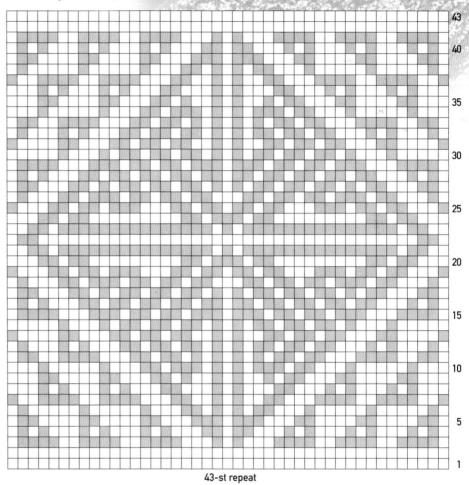

43-st repeat

Work k1b, p1 rib: 3 rnds **A**, 1 rnd **B**, 1 rnd **D**, 3 rnds **A**.

Chart: With **C**, k rnd 1, inc to 86 sts as foll: *K1, [BL1, k1]
21 times; rep from*. Work through chart rnd 43 with **E** on
C ground.

Edging: *K1 rnd, p 1 rnd with **B**; rep from* with **A**. Bind off
purlwise with **A**.

COLORS

A Black

B Blue

C Purple

D Green

E Yellow

Here is a mitten without a long cuff, though it could have any you wanted. The last three 6-row pattern repeats form the cuff which is made smaller by using a smaller sized needle and decreasing the band over two rounds to eliminate 6 stitches. Any small repeat pattern could be cuffed in this manner.

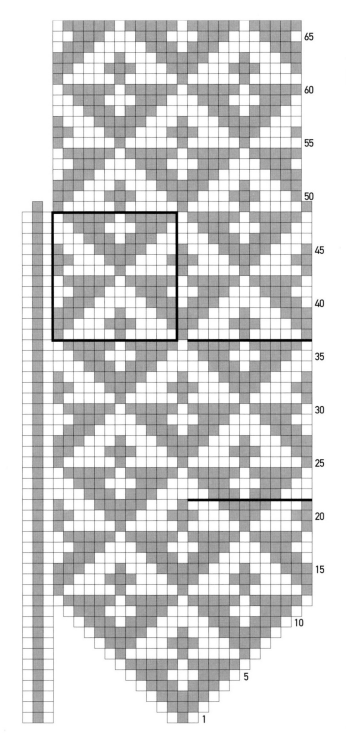

MITTEN

Follow General Directions for Mitten with Striped Band and work through row 48 of Mitten chart, using photo as guide for colors. Follow cuff instructions for wrist shaping.

CUFF

Change to smaller needles. Continue in pattern but decrease the band over rnds 49 and 50 as follows: K last pattern st tog with first band st, k center band st, ssk last band st with first pattern st; repeat on other side. On next rnd, k remaining band st tog with last pattern st. Work to top of chart.

Edging: With **A**, work attached I-cord edge.

COLORS

A Tan

Small amounts (6 yards each will do 6 rnds, half a repeat) of various colors

5 | large-patterned mittens

Large-patterned mittens are made much the same way as small-patterned mittens. The only difference is in working the thumb. Here you must draw the vertical line on your chart joining the row at the tip of the thumb and that at the base. This gives you a small chart for the thumb, 12 stitches wide and 15–17 rows long. To work around the thumb, begin this small chart at the right side. Work to the left side. Then work back from left to right. This brings you back to the start of the round. Continue through the rounds of the thumb chart.

Large patterns have more scope for variety than small ones, but they are not necessarily more attractive. I usually find myself wanting simpler cuffs with the larger patterns on the mittens.

Since the thumb is worked separately, you may want to cut off about ten yards of each color before you start the mitten. Then you won't have to cut the working yarns when you get to the thumb. On the other hand if you're going to follow my placement of the thumb, with the blind faith that it will fit your hand too, you can make the thumb first. Then it's ready to insert when you get there.

All the large-patterned mittens follow the general directions in Chapter 3 for materials and methods. Begin with plain (p. 26) or striped band (p. 30). This is indicated at the top of each set of instructions. For any unfamiliar techniques or abbreviations, see Chapter 9, p. 132. See Chapter 7, p. 126 for edge finishes and Chapter 8, p. 130 to add a warm and voluptuous lining.

Feel free to vary embellishments, edgings, and colors, not to mention using nubbly or rainbow-dyed yarn. Furthermore, all the mittens in this chapter are decreased to 44 stitches at the wrist, so any of the cuffs can be knit onto any of the mittens

*Being short,
these mittens are in
greater danger than most
of one mitten's getting lost.
So I have knitted in a
button and loop at the
edge to keep them
together at least.*

   *This pattern is quite easy
to follow but not easy to
learn. I don't know why.*

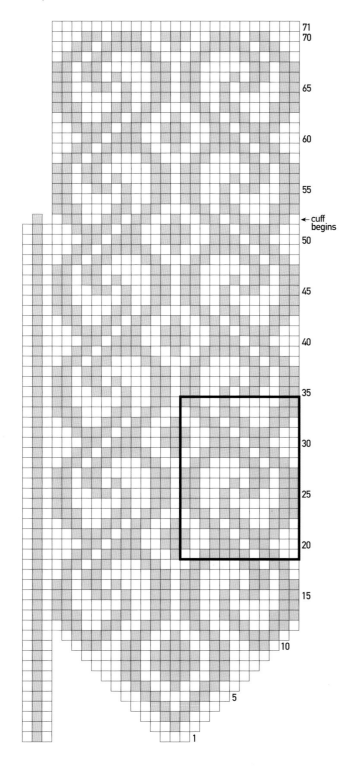

MITTEN

Follow General Directions for Mitten with Striped Band and work through row 51 of chart. Follow cuff instructions for wrist shaping. Make the second mitten with colors **C** and **B**, instead of **A** and **B**.

CUFF

Additional yarns **70 yds C** (used in mitten and cuff); **7 yds D**

On rnd 52, change to smaller needles and work sl2-k1-p2sso at each side edge. On chart row 53, work k2tog at each side edge. Work to top of chart.

With **D**, k 1 rnd.

Edging: With **D**, work attached I-cord with loop and button.

COLORS

A Blue

B Pink

C Green

D Orange

A surprisingly easy
and satisfying pattern to
work. The third color on the
mitten is done in duplicate
stitch. It could be easily knit
in by carrying the yarn
vertically down the inside of
the mitten. The advantage
of duplicate stitch here is
that you don't have to
decide what color you want
to use—or if you want any
at all—until you can see the
whole mitten.

MITTEN

Follow General Directions for Mitten with Plain Band and
work to top of Mitten chart.

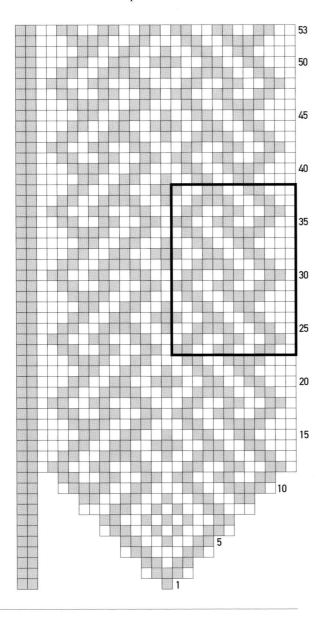

CUFF

Additional yarns **50g C; 30 yds each of D and F; 25 yds E**

Work k1b, p1 rib: 3 rnds **A**, 2 rnds **C**.

With **C**, k 2 rnds, inc to 84 sts on first rnd as foll: *K2, [M1, k1]
20 times; rep from*.

Chart 1: Work 16 rnds in chart pat with **E** and **D** on **C** ground.

Chart 2: Work 4 rnds in chart pat with **A** and **B**.

With **C**, k 2 rnds, inc 12 sts on rnd 2 as
foll: *K7, M1; rep from*.

Chart 1: Rep chart 1 with **F** and **D** on
C ground.

Edging: Work ball fringe edge.

12-st repeat

4-st repeat

COLORS

A Violet

B Orange

C Magenta

D Green

E Chartreuse

F Blue

Though this is a Turkish pattern, it makes me think of Easter eggs, hence the decoration. But it's a fine pattern without embroidery too. Like most Turkish patterns, it's simple and pleasant to work.

MITTEN

Follow General Directions for Mitten with Striped Band and work to
top of Mitten chart. Using photo as guide, duplicate stitch the back of
the mitten and work Palestrina knots in **G**.

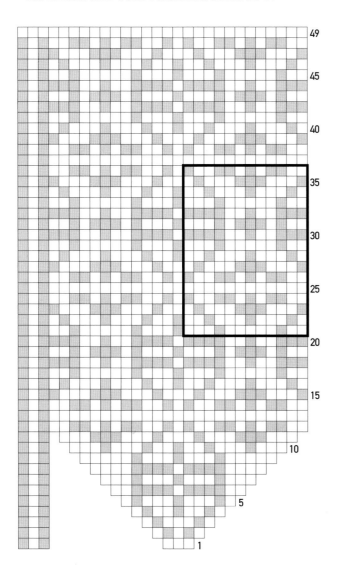

CUFF

Additional yarns **50g A**; **25 yds each of C, D, E and E**

Work wrist ridge: Rnds 1–2 With **A**, purl. **Rnd 3** With **C**, *k1, sl 1 with
yarn in back (wyib); rep from*. **Rnd 4** With **C**, *p1, sl 1 wyib; rep from*.
Rnd 5 With **A**, knit. **Rnds 6–7** With **A**, purl. **Rnd 8** With **A**, k and inc to 64
sts as foll: *K2, [BL1, k2]10 times; rep from*.

****Chart:** With **C** on **A** ground, work 9 rnds in chart pat.

Work cuff ridge: Rnd 1 With **A**, *k3, lifted inc in next st; rep from*. **Rnd 2**
K1A, k1B; rep from. **Rnd 3** *K1A, p1B; rep from*. **Rnd 4** With **A**, knit.**

Rep between ***'s working chart with **D** on **A** ground.

Rep between ***'s working chart with **E** on **A** ground and working inc's
every 8th st on rnd 1 of cuff ridge.

Rep between ***'s working chart with **F** on **A** ground.

Chart: With **F** on **A** ground, work 9 rnds in chart pat.

Edging: Work wool beads edge with **A** and **G**.

Note: On the 2nd cuff, use photo as guide to colors.

4-st repeat

COLORS

A Dark green

B Light green

C Gold

D Blue

E Purple

F Red

G Pink

5 | 4

*This pattern is as
simple as many of the
small repeats. It is,
however, a 14-stitch repeat
and does not fit evenly into
the 24-stitch thumb. Hence
each row of the thumb
chart must be worked from
R to L and L to R. Because
it is so simple, it lends itself
to various embellishments.
I've added rose beads to
the mitten and cuff edge.
One could also fill the
squares with Palestrina
knots or with Smyrna
crosses. When embroidering
on knitting, you can try
anything and if you don't
like it, take it out without
leaving a trace.*

*I have reversed colors
A and B on the second
mitten for a little variation.
There's no need to do this
if you'd rather not.*

MITTEN

Follow General Directions for Mitten with Striped Band and work to top of Mitten chart. Before beginning to knit, string 10 beads on **A**. Work beads into the back of the mitten only (not the palm) where indicated on the chart.

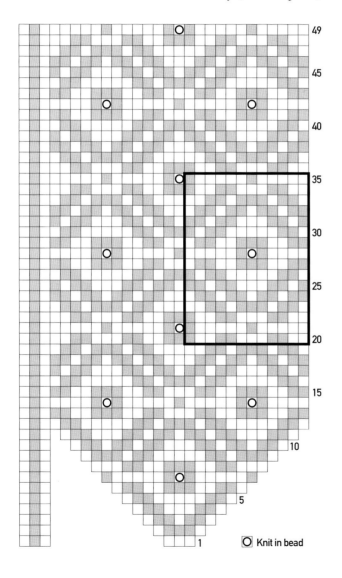

	O Knit in bead

CUFF

Additional materials **90 yds C; 85 yds D**

Optional **86 gold rose beads (for back of hand and cuff)**

Work k1b, p1 rib: 3 rnds B, 2 rnds C, 3 rnds B.

With **C**, k 2 rnds, inc to 69 sts on first rnd as foll: [K1, BL1] 3 times, [k2, BL1] 10 times; [k1, BL1] 3 times; [k2, BL1] 9 times.

Chart 1: Work 3 rnds of chart with **A** on **C** ground. With **C**, k 2 rnds, inc to 92 sts on first rnd as foll: *K3, BL1; rep from*.

Chart 2: Work 15 rnds of chart with **D** on **C** ground. With **C**, k 2 rnds, inc to 99 sts on rnd 2 as foll: [BL1, k13] 6 times; BL1, k14.

Chart 1: Work 3 rnds of chart with **B** on **C** ground. With **C**, k 2 rnds.

Edging: With **D**, work fat beaded fringe edge.

1

3

1

3-st repeat

2

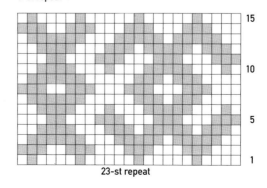

23-st repeat

COLORS

A Teal

B Purple

C Orange

D Yellow

A thin, simple pattern seems to ask for complexity in the ground, hence 3-round stripes of different colors. This would be a good design for using up small bits of yarn: each stripe will take no more than two yards. To knit them with three background colors as shown here, you will need about 35 yards of each color (that will include the cuff) and a 50g ball of the pattern color.

MITTEN

Follow General Directions for Mitten with Striped Band
and work to top of Mitten chart. Dotted lines on the chart
indicate that the ground color alternates: **A, C, D.**

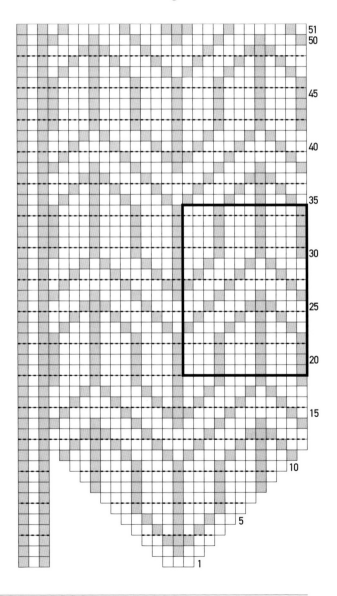

CUFF

Additional yarns **50g E; 45 yards each of C and D (used for mitten and cuff)**

Work k1b, p1 rib: 3 rnds **D**, 2 rnds **B**, 3 rnds **A**.

With **E**, k 1 rnd, inc to 80 sts as foll: *K4, [BL1, k1] 18 times; rep from*.

Chart: Work 9 rnds in chart pat with **C on **E** ground.

Work ridge with B: Rnd 1 Knit. **Rnd 2** K into front and back of each st
around. **Rnd 3** P2tog around.******

With **E**, k 1 rnd, inc to 88 sts as foll: *K10, BL1; rep from*.

Rep between ******'s, working chart with **D** on **E** ground.

With **E**, inc to 96 sts as foll: *K11, BL1; rep from*.

Rep between ******'s, working chart with **A** on **E** ground.

Edging: With **E**, work fringe edge.

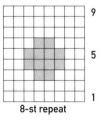

8-st repeat

COLORS

A Magenta

B Yellow

C Green

D Violet

E Black

*Here is a
conservative mitten,
perhaps for your favorite
banker or attorney. It's a
very simple 10-stitch repeat,
the same on both cuff and
mitten. I've tried to jazz up
this pattern in a number of
ways but it has always
looked better plain. Still, it's
one of my favorites.*

MITTEN

Follow General Directions for Mitten with Striped Band and
work to top of Mitten chart.

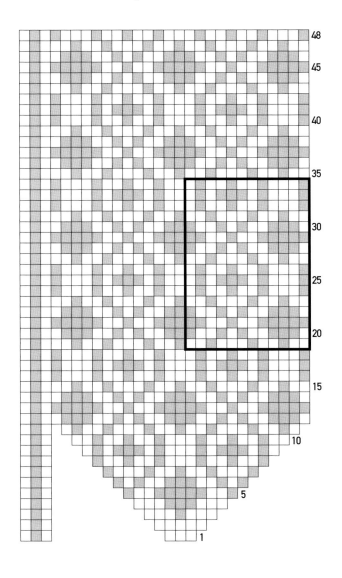

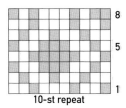

CUFF

Additional yarns: **50g each A and C**

Work k1b, p1 rib: 5 rnds with **A**.

With **A**, k 1 rnd, inc to 80 sts as foll: *K4, [M1, k1] 18 times;
rep from*.

Chart: With **C** on **A** ground, work 32 rnds in chart pat.

Edging: With **A**, work fringe edge.

10-st repeat

COLORS

A Purple

B Light orange

C Dark orange

This started out as an 11-row Fair Isle pattern from Sheila McGregor's, The Complete Book of Fair Isle Knitting (see chart below). I turned it 90°, changed a few stitches, and added side pieces—an easy and pleasing mitten design technique. Fair Isle patterns worked in two colors seem to beg for embellishment—more fun and games, if you like doing it.

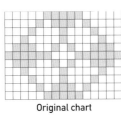

Original chart

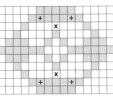

+ Changed to pattern
x Changed to ground

MITTEN

Follow General Directions for Mitten with Plain Band and work to top of
Mitten chart. Colors **C** and **D** are optional embellishments to be added later.
Using photo as guide, work duplicate st in **C** and Smyrna cross st in **D**.

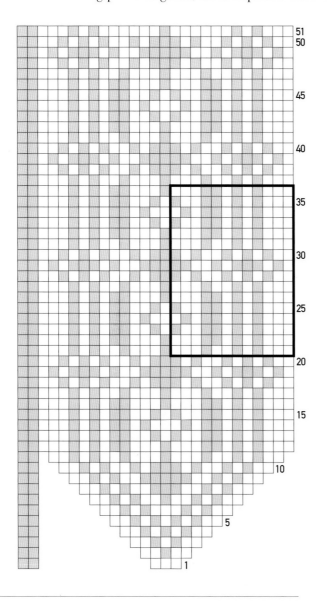

CUFF

Additional yarns **50g A; 35 yds each of C and D**

Work k1b, p1 rib: 4 rnds **A**, 2 rnds **D**.

With **A**, k 2 rnds, inc on first rnd to 80 sts as foll: *K4, [BL1, k1]
18 times; rep from*.

Chart: Work 11 rnds in chart pat with **C and **D** on **A** ground. With
A, k 3 rnds, inc to 90 sts on 3rd rnd as foll: *K8, M1; rep from*.

Rep chart with **B** and **C** on **A** ground and 2 sts between I-motifs. With
A k 3 rnds, inc to 100 sts on 3rd rnd as foll: *K9, M1; rep from*.

Work chart with **D** and **B** on **A** ground and 3 sts between I-motifs.
With **A**, k 3 rnds.

Edging: With **C**, k 1 rnd, then work 4 rnds in k1b, p1 rib.
Work tubular bind-off.

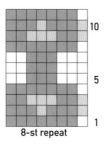

8-st repeat

COLORS

A Green

B Light yellow

C Orange

D Purple

This pattern, worked in gold or silver, makes a fine evening mitten. It isn't easy to follow, but sometimes one wants a challenge. The cuff, on the other hand, is extremely simple and would look well on almost any mitten. The finishing is yet another matter. There are lots of ends, but there are tubes to run them into. It makes up slowly, but it is beautiful.

MITTEN

Follow General Directions for Mitten with Plain Band and work to top of Mitten chart, reversing colors on second mitten.

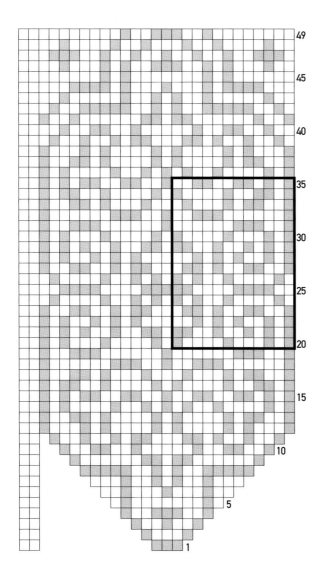

CUFF

Additional yarns **50g C; 70 yds each A and B (or 50g of the color you use as ground if you are not going to reverse colors)**

Note: When 2 colors are given, use the first for the first mitten and 2nd color (in parenthesis) for the 2nd mitten.

Work k1b, p1 rib: 3 rnds **A (B)**, 2 rnds **C**, 3 rnds **A (B)**.

With **A (B)**, k 1 rnd, inc to 66 sts as foll: *K2, M1; rep from*.

Chart: Work 40 rnds in chart pat with **C** on **A (B)** ground. On inc rnds 4, 13, 22, and 31, work backward loop inc (BL1) as indicated on chart—8 incs per rnd.

With **A (B)**, k 1 rnd.

Edging: With **B (A)**, work looped I-cord edge.

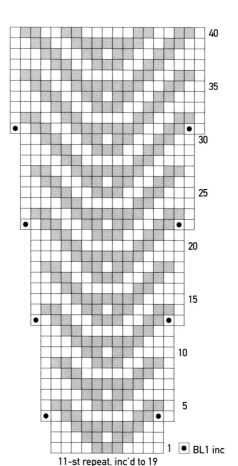

11-st repeat, inc'd to 19

● BL1 inc

COLORS

A Purple

B Blue

C Green

When I made this
mitten, I began with three
stitches and increased to
27 on front and back
instead of the more usual
beginning with five stitches
and increasing to 25.
There's no reason not to
make the usual 3-stitch
band. It would incorporate
the last stitch of each side.

MITTEN

Follow General Directions for Mitten with Plain Band, wrapping 3 sts instead of 5, and work to top of Mitten chart. Dotted lines on the chart indicate that the pattern color alternates from **A** to **C**; this changes color of "plain" band. Follow cuff instructions for wrist shaping.

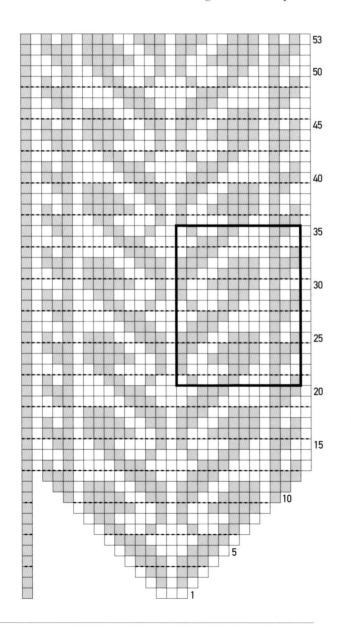

CUFF

Additional yarns **50g C (used in mitten and cuff)**

Change to needles 2 sizes smaller.

Work chart: Rnd 1: With **B** on **A** ground, work in chart pat and dec as foll: *K6, [k2tog] 8 times, k6; rep from*. Work 7 more rnds in chart pat with **B** on **A** ground, then work 8 rnds with **C** on **A** ground.

Edging: With **C**, k 1 rnd, then work 4 rnds in k1b, p1 rib. Work tubular bind-off.

RIGHT

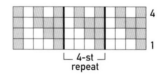

4

1

└ 4-st ┘
repeat

LEFT

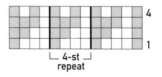

4

1

└ 4-st ┘
repeat

COLORS

A White

B Violet

C Blue

This began as a fairly standard 25-row Fair Isle pattern (see below). I centered the pattern vertically between half patterns because of the tip shaping, then I changed the corner pattern into a connecting line. The pattern, as it worked up, looked uninteresting to me, so I added Palestrina knots with duplicate stitch. The finished mitten back, compared to the palm side, demonstrates what a difference a little embroidery can make.

Original chart with tip marked in heavy line
⊞ Changed to pattern   ☒ Changed to ground

MITTEN

Follow General Directions for Mitten with Striped Band and work to top of
Mitten chart. Work duplicate st and Palestrina knots in **C** as indicated on chart.

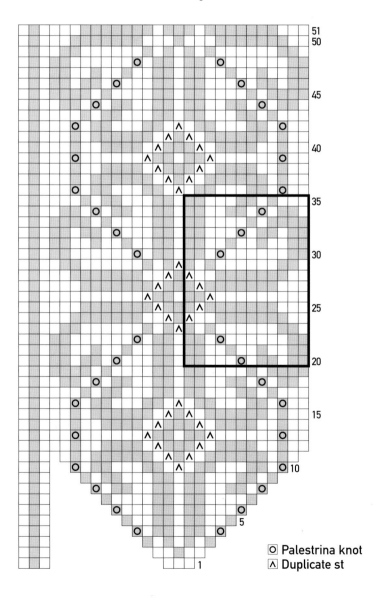

☉ Palestrina knot
⋀ Duplicate st

CUFF

Additional yarns **30 yds C; 50g D**

Work k1b, p1 rib: 3 rnds **A**, 2 rnds **C**, 3 rnds **D**.

With **D**, k 1 rnd, inc to 84 sts as foll: *K2, [M1, k1] 20 times; rep from*.

Chart 1: With **D** on **A** ground, work 24 rnds in chart pat. With **A**, k 1
rnd, then p 3 rnds. With **B**, k 2 rnds.

Chart 2: Work 8 chart rnds with **C** on **B** ground. K 2 rnds **B**.

Edging: Work double roll edge as foll: With **A**, k 1 rnd, p 3 rnds. With
D, k 2 rnds, p 3 rnds. With **D**, bind off purlwise.

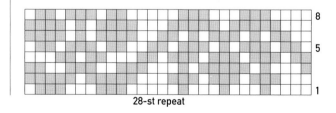

COLORS

A Green

B Pink

C Orange

D Purple

This is basically an extremely simple pattern which, if extended to a large size (such as a sweater or pillow) is monotonous to work. However, at this scale it is a little tricky to find a comfortable rhythm to work it in because the 8-stitch pattern does not repeat before coming to the center. It is nevertheless one of my favorites. I put it with a lace cuff because it looked delicate and lacy to me in these colors. Bright colors with a sharp contrast make a big difference.

MITTEN

Follow General Directions for Mitten with Plain Band and
work to top of Mitten chart. When shaping wrist, decrease to
40 stitches.

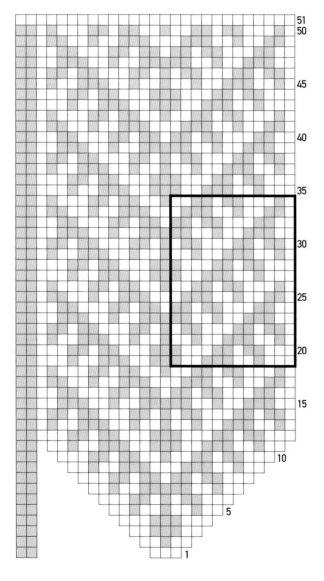

CUFF

Additional yarns **50g C**

Work wrist ridge: Change to smaller needles and **C**. [K 1 rnd, p 1
rnd] twice. K 1 rnd, inc to 80 sts as foll: *K1, M1; rep from*.

Work lace pat: Rnd 1 *Ssk, k4, yo, k1, yo, k4, k2tog, k3; rep from*
around. **Rnds 2, 4, 6, 8, 10** Knit. **Rnd 3** *Ssk, [k3, yo] twice, k3,
k2tog, k3; rep from* around. **Rnd 5** *Ssk, k2, yo, k2tog, yo, k1, yo,
ssk, yo, k2, k2tog, k3; rep from* around. **Rnd 7** *Ssk, k1, yo, k2tog,
yo, k3, yo, ssk, yo, k1, k2tog, k3; rep from* around. **Rnd 9** *Ssk, yo,
[k2tog, yo] twice, k1, [yo, ssk] twice, yo, k2tog, k3; rep from*
around. **Rnds 11, 13** *P13, k3; rep from* around. **Rnd 12** *K14,
lifted inc, k2; rep from* around.

Work 13 rnds of lace pat twice more. Note that because of incs on
rnd 12, there will be one more stitch in the stockinette stitch panels
with each repeat.

Edging: With **B**, k 1 rnd, then p 1 rnd. With **A**,
k 1 rnd, then bind off purlwise.

COLORS

A Light green

B Pink

C Medium green

Here is another Fair Isle pattern. This time it's an 11-row pattern set vertically and repeated twice with one stitch on each side and one stitch between. It looked good on paper but I didn't like it much knitted up (see palm of mitten). So I began to embroider with the resultant back, that I like a lot. My designing philosophy tends to be: if you don't like what you've done, keep adding until it pleases you. This doesn't suit everybody, but I urge you to give it a try. It's much more fun than failure and you learn a lot doing it.

MITTEN

Follow General Directions for Mitten with Plain Band and work to top of Mitten chart. Using photo and chart as guide, work embellishment following key below.

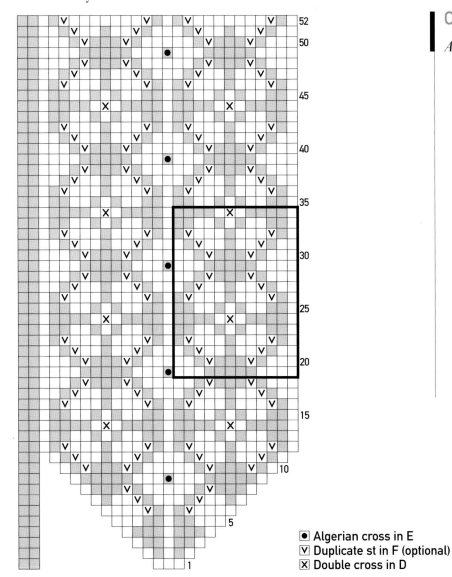

CUFF

Additional yarns 50g C; 30 yds D; 35 yds each of E and F

Work wrist pat: Rnds 1–2 With A, k 1 rnd, then p 1 rnd. **Rnd 3** With B, *k1, sl 1 with yarn in back (wyib); rep from*. **Rnd 4** With B, *p1, sl 1 wyib; rep from*. **Rnds 5–6** With A, rep rnds 1–2. **Rnd 7** With A, k1 rnd, inc to 64 sts as foll: *K2 , [M1, k2] 10 times; rep from*.

Rnds 8–17 *K2C, k2D; rep from* around.

Rnds 18–24 Rep rnds 1–7 of wrist pat, inc to 80 sts on last rnd as foll: *K4, M1; rep from*.

Rnds 25–36 *K2C, k2E; rep from* around.

Rnds 37–43 Rep rnds 1–7 of wrist pat, inc to 96 sts on last rnd as foll: *K5, M1; rep from*.

Rnds 44–57 *K2C, k2F; rep from* around.

Rnds 58–63 Rep rnds 1–6 of wrist pat.

Edging: With B, work fringe edge.

● Algerian cross in E
V Duplicate st in F (optional)
X Double cross in D

COLORS

A Blue

B Tan

C Dark tan

D Red

E Dark green

F Purple

Here is a traditional Eastern sock turned mitten. I wanted to do something with it, but it was too strong a pattern to alter effectively. The cuff looks rather simpler than it is, since there are three rounds that have three colors in them. Three colors are a lot more work than two—but there are only three rounds.

MITTEN

Follow General Directions for Mitten with Striped Band and
work to top of Mitten chart.

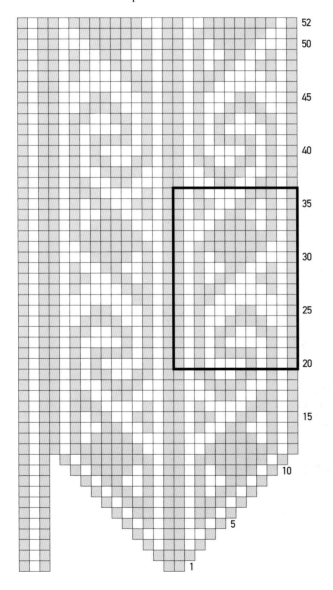

CUFF

Additional yarns **50g C**; **25 yds each of D and E**

Work k1b, p1 rib: With **A**, work 6 rnds.

With **C**, k 1 rnd, inc to 60 sts as foll: *K6, [BL1, k2] 8 times;
rep from*.

Work chart: Work 35 rnds in chart pat with
D, **A**, **E**, then **B** on **C** ground. On inc rnds 8,
16, and 24, work backward loop inc (BL1) as
indicated on chart—12 incs per rnd.

Edging: With **A** and **B**, work braid edge.

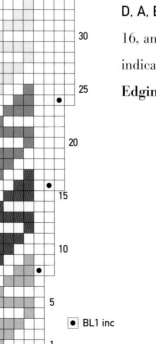

● BL1 inc

5-st repeat, inc'd to 8

COLORS

A Purple

B Green

C Tan

D Orange

E Pink

This is essentially the same pattern as 5-07 and 5-12 enlarged a bit with minor changes. A whole different look and one that, at least to my eye, does not want further embellishment.

MITTEN

Follow General Directions for Mitten with Plain Band and
work to top of Mitten chart. Work second mitten with color **C**
instead of **B**.

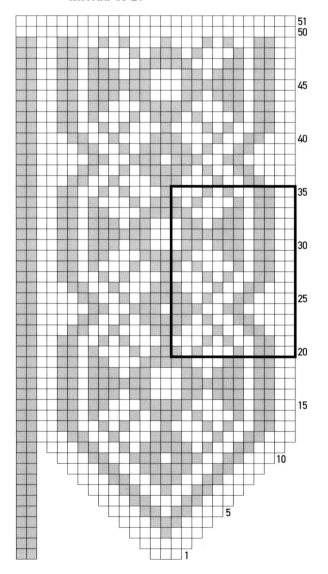

CUFF

Additional yarns **50g C** (for mitten and cuff); **50g D**

Note: When 2 colors are given, use the first on one mitten and 2nd
(in parenthesis) on the 2nd mitten.

Work k1b, p1 rib: 3 rnds **B (C)**, 2 rnds **D**, 3 rnds **B (C)**.

With **D**, k 3 rnds, inc to 78 sts on first rnd as foll: *K5, [BL1, k1] 17
times; rep from*.

Chart 1: Work 11 rnds in chart pat using **C (B)** for rnds 1–5 and
7–11, and **B (C)** for rnd 6, all on a **D**
ground. With **D**, k 3 rnds, inc on 3rd
rnd to 96 sts as foll: *K3, [M1, k4] 9
times; rep from*.

Chart 2: Work 3 rnds in chart pat with
A on **D** ground. With **D**, k 3 rnds.

Chart 3: Work 11 rnds in chart pat in
same colors as chart 1. With **D**, k 3 rnds.

Edging: With **A**,
work attached
I-cord edge.

1

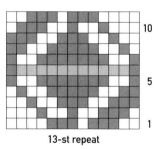

13-st repeat

2

4-st repeat

3

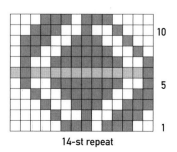

14-st repeat

COLORS

A Gold

B Red

C Purple

D Black

This mitten is quite discreet done as it is in dark colors. If you used royal blue and gold and filled the pattern centers with scarlet, it would turn flamboyant.

MITTEN

Follow General Directions for Mitten with Plain Band and
work to top of Mitten chart.

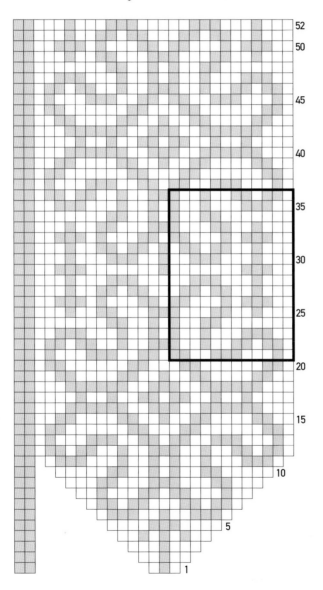

CUFF

Additional yarns 50g C; 25 yds each of C, D, and E

Work k1b, p1 rib: 3 rnds A.

Chart: Work 40 rnds in chart pat, working with
A, E, B, D, and A on C ground. Inc as indicated
on rnds 8, 17, 28, and 37. A lifted increase is the
least noticeable, especially if it is done in the
middle of the strip of C instead of at the side.

Edging: With A, work fringe edge.

● Lifted inc

2-st repeat,
inc'd to 6

COLORS

A Dark green

B Purple

C Rust

D Light green

E Pink

This is a mitten for those who want a challenge. There are two patterns repeating with different numbers of rows. The sides, mirror images, are an 8-stitch, 7-round pattern, the center a 9-stitch, 11-round pattern.

Once you catch on to the pattern and can work it with a minimum of errors (I confess I took out half the rounds I knit), it seems a shame to stop. So I made these long under-sleeve mittens with no pattern change.

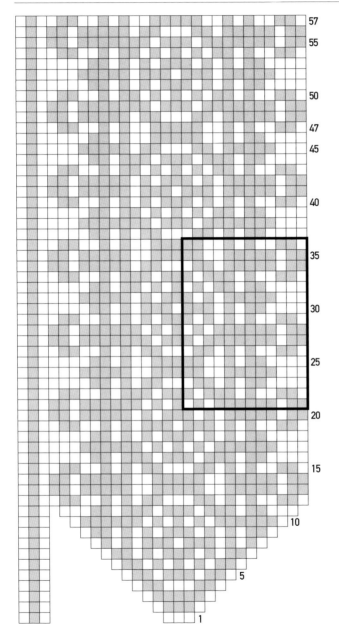

MITTEN

Follow General Directions for Mitten with Striped Band and work to top of Mitten chart. Omit wrist shaping. Work 2nd mitten with **C** instead of **B**.

CUFF

Additional yarns **50g C (used for 2nd mitten and cuff)**

Change to needles 2 sizes smaller.

Chart: Work 22 rnds of chart, continuing colors as for mitten.

Edging: Work attached I-cord with **C** for one mitten; with **B** for 2nd mitten.

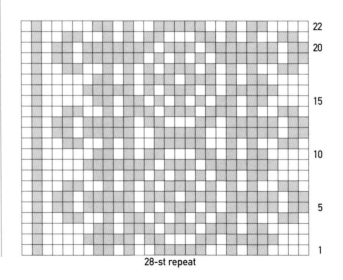

28-st repeat

COLORS

A Light blue

B Pink

C Purple

Here is a child's mitten. This pattern comes from Caucasian carpets. Although many Eastern knitting patterns are taken from carpets, I've never seen this one knit. It seems a bit odd since it's extremely knittable—one of those patterns learned after the first time through. I've made the cuff equally simple on the grounds that children's mittens should not be a major undertaking: they don't last long enough.

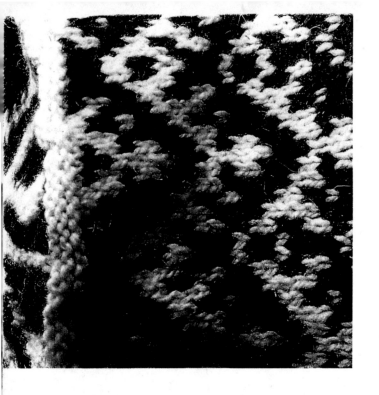

My dictionary (*The American Heritage Dictionary of the English Language*) defines a toque as a small, brimless, close-fitting woman's hat. The hats I've given here differ from most close-fitting, contemporary hats in two ways. First, the top is separated from the bottom by a band that causes the top to lie flat. Second, the bottom is slightly tapered. Tapering the bottom limits the patterns that can be used but makes for a more graceful, comfortable fit.

Directions

On smaller, 16-inch (41 cm) circular needle, cast on 96 sts. Work desired band. (Band A is shown on hat #1; band B on hat #s 2, 3, and 4; and band C on hat #5).

Follow the bottom chart, using a lifted increase where increases are shown.

When you have completed the chart, work the band again (now on 120 sts).

Work the top chart. Use the double decrease on hat #s 1, 2, and 4. Use R-slanting dec at beginning and L-slanting dec at ending of chart segments on hat #4. Use R-slanting dec at end of chart segment on hat #5.

When the chart is finished, run end of yarn through remaining sts and pull tight.

Blocking

The bottom of this hat can be steamed over the tip of an ironing board or sleeve board. The top can be steamed over a 9-inch (23 cm) plate or a 9-inch circle of Masonite or cardboard.

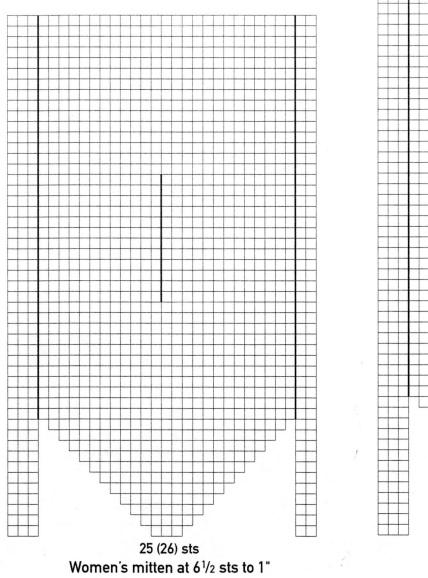

25 (26) sts
Women's mitten at 6½ sts to 1"

31 (32) sts
Man's mitten at 6½ sts to 1"

MITTEN

Follow General Directions for Mitten with Plain Band and work to top of Mitten chart. When shaping wrist, decrease to 32 stitches. Using photo as guide and with **C**, work stem st on back of hand along vertical stripes and across tip.

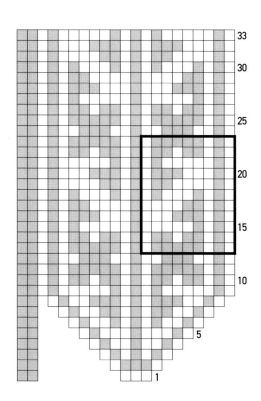

CUFF

Additional yarns **30 yds C**

Work cuff ridge: With **A**, [k 1 rnd, p 1 rnd] 3 times.

With **B**, k 1 rnd, inc to 48 sts as foll: *K2, BL1; rep from*.

Chart: Work 5 rnds in chart pat with **C on **B** ground.

Rnd 6 With **B**, k 1 rnd, inc to 60 sts as foll: *K4, BL1; rep from*.

Rnds 7-8 With **A**, k 1 rnd, p 1 rnd. **Rnd 9** With **B**, k 1 rnd.**

Rep between **'s and with **B**, inc to 72 sts on rnd 6 as foll: *K5, BL1; rep from*.

Rep between **'s once more but do not work any incs on rnd 6.

Edging: With **A**, [k 1 rnd, p 1 rnd] 3 times. Bind off purlwise with **A**.

6-st repeat

COLORS

A Green

B Yellow

C Purple

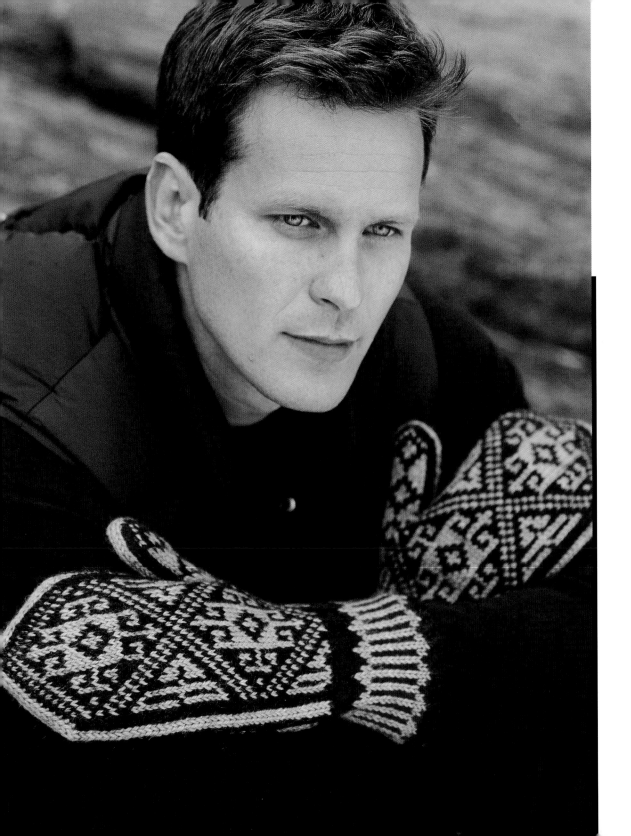

6 | sore-thumb mittens

Some people prefer mittens with the thumb sticking out the side. It is for them that this chapter is written. It should be noted, however, that all but the last two mittens in this collection could be made with the invisible thumb: just mark the thumb on the chart where you want it and follow the directions in Chapter 3. It further should be noted that any of the invisible-thumb mittens can be converted to sore-thumb mittens, though this would take a little more work. You would have to chart a thumb pattern the way you want it and add it into the mitten chart. A blank thumb chart is here for the copying (see p. 138) to make this less onerous.

You will see, of course, that these directions are not markedly different from those for invisible-thumb mittens except from thumb to wrist. The beginning is exactly the same, though in many cases the number of stitches in the band will be more than three. It generally works better for sore-thumb mittens to have a broader band since the thumb is inserted across the side of the mitten and only the band stitches are knitted together with thumb stitches. Also, in some cases the mitten is worked so that the band goes over the top of the hand from back to palm. In these cases the band carries the main pattern. The charts show the number of band stitches after the shaping for the mitten tip is complete, so when you start, remember to cast on two stitches in addition to the band stitches shown on the chart.

All the sore-thumb mittens follow the general directions in Chapter 3 for materials and methods. Following any special directions at the top of each set of instructions, begin with plain (p. 26) or striped band (p. 30). This is indicated at the top of each set of instructions. For any unfamiliar techniques or abbreviations, see Chapter 9, p. 132. See Chapter 7, p. 126 for edge finishes and Chapter 8, p. 130 to add a warm and voluptuous lining.

Feel free to vary embellishments, edgings, and colors, not to mention using nubbly or rainbow-dyed yarn. Furthermore, all the mittens in this chapter are decreased to 44 stitches at the wrist, so any of the cuffs can be knit onto any of the mittens.

This mitten pattern is taken from another pattern: the between parts of mitten 5-3. There are quite a few long carries here, but they're easy ones. What makes an "easy carry"? The difficult part of carrying yarn is doing it in such a way that it does not show on the right side. When there is a stitch on the preceding round in the color that is to be carried, and it occurs where you want to catch the stitches, carrying is easy: you catch the stitches here and the color never shows through.

Chart row 4 shows an "easy" carry across 9 stitches. The carried yarn can be caught above the center stitch or the pattern stitch to either side of it.

THUMB

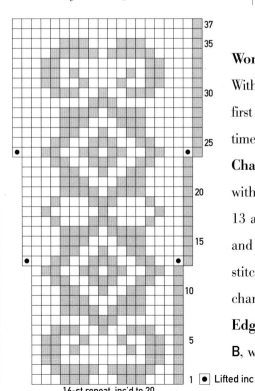

MITTEN

Follow General Directions for Sore-Thumb Mitten and work to top of Mitten and Thumb charts.

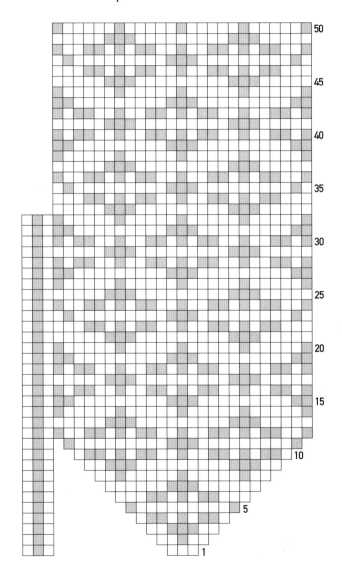

CUFF

Additional yarns **50g** each of **A** and **C**

Work k1b, p1 rib: 4 rnds **B**.
With **C**, k 3 rnds, inc to 80 sts on first rnd as foll: *K2, [BL1, k1] 18 times, end k2; rep from*.

Chart: Work 37 rnds of cuff chart with **A** on **C** ground. On inc rnds 13 and 24, work lifted inc before and after single **A** stitch as indicated on chart—10 incs per rnd.

Edging: With **A** and **B**, work braid.

16-st repeat, inc'd to 20

COLORS

A Red

B Light green

C Dark green

1 ● Lifted inc

$6 \Big|^2$

The cuff on this mitten uses a technique named "motif intarsia" by Priscilla Gibson-Roberts. I've also heard it called tapestry knitting. See p. 109 for directions. Although one could, with this technique, knit in all the colors, I only did the green and put the others in with duplicate stitch. It's a little slow to do—one of those things that's fun if you like it and painful if you don't. It might be worthwhile trying a swatch before plunging into the whole thing.

MITTEN

Begin as noted below and follow General Directions for Sore-Thumb Mitten, working to top of Mitten and Thumb charts.

Note: Begin with back loop cast-on, casting on 7 sts in **A. Row 1** K2A, 1D, 1A, 1D, 2A. **Row 2** Purl back with **A.** Rep row 1 with the tail of **D.** Rep row 2. Pick up around the rectangle on the next rnd. Begin the thumb the same way, but pick up around the rectangle after row 2.

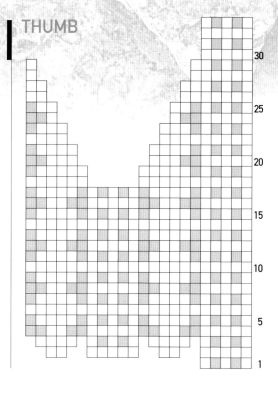

THUMB

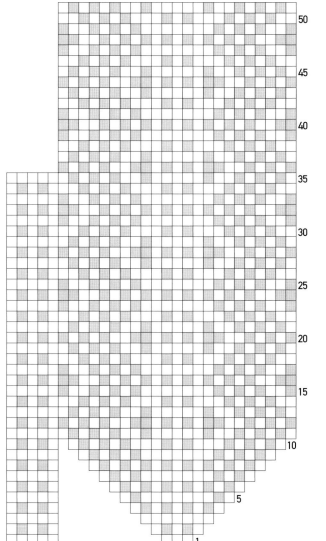

CUFF

Additional materials **Approximately 60 yds each of A, B, C; 35 yds E; 20 yds D; 16" circular needle**

Work **k1b, p1 rib:** 4 rnds **A**, 2 rnds **D**, 4 rnds **A**.

With **B**, k 2 rnds, inc to 84 sts on first rnd as foll: *K2, [k1, BL1] 20 times; rep from*.

Chart: (See next page for cuff charts.) Using circular needle and Motif intarsia, work 40 rows of 40-st left (or right) cuff chart, centering it on the back of the hand. Work rows 1–16 with **E** on **B** ground, change the ground to **C** after rnd 13, and to **A** after rnd 27.

Edging: With **A** and **D**, work braid edge. With **C**, work fringe edge.

Embellish: Using photo as guide, work duplicate stitch in **D**, **A**, and **B**. Work eye in Palestrina knot in **D**.

COLORS

A Red

B Purple

C Blue

D Orange

E Green

These mittens could equally well be done with an invisible thumb since they have only a 2-stitch band. I've reversed the colors on the second mitten but that's certainly not necessary.

MITTEN

Begin as noted below and follow General Directions for Sore-Thumb Mitten, working to top of Mitten and Thumb charts.

Note: Begin with back loop cast-on, casting on 7 sts in **A**. **Row 1** K2A, 1D, 1A, 1D, 2A. **Row 2** Purl back with **A**. Rep row 1 with the tail of **D**. Rep row 2. Pick up around the rectangle on the next rnd. Begin the thumb the same way, but pick up around the rectangle after row 2.

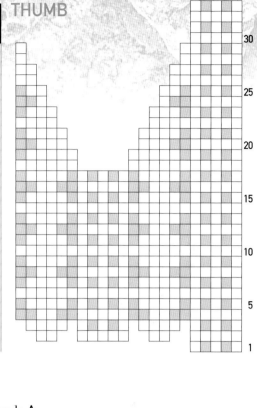

THUMB

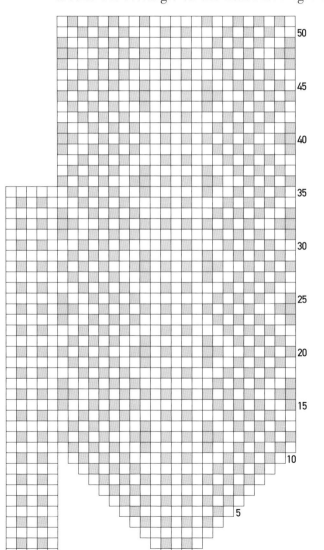

CUFF

Additional materials **Approximately 60 yds each of A, B, C; 35 yds E; 20 yds D; 16" circular needle**

Work k1b, p1 rib: 4 rnds A, 2 rnds D, 4 rnds A.

With **B**, k 2 rnds, inc to 84 sts on first rnd as foll: *K2, [k1, BL1] 20 times; rep from*.

Chart: (See next page for cuff charts.) Using circular needle and Motif intarsia, work 40 rows of 40-st left (or right) cuff chart, centering it on the back of the hand. Work rows 1–16 with **E** on **B** ground, change the ground to **C** after rnd 13, and to **A** after rnd 27.

Edging: With **A** and **D**, work braid edge. With **C**, work fringe edge.

Embellish: Using photo as guide, work duplicate stitch in **D**, **A**, and **B**. Work eye in Palestrina knot in **D**.

COLORS

A Red

B Purple

C Blue

D Orange

E Green

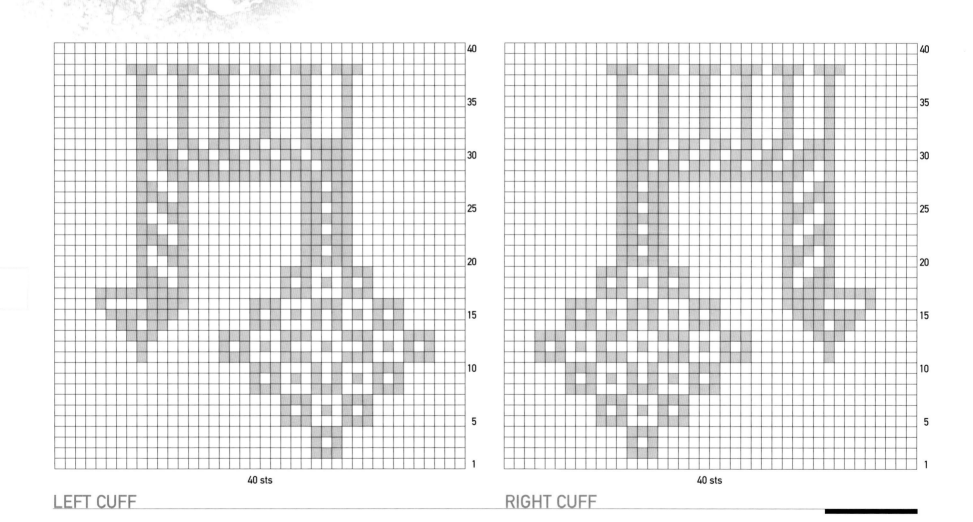

LEFT CUFF   RIGHT CUFF

motif intarsia worked on a circular needle

Rnd A

1. Strand pattern color and ground color across motif stitches.

2. Drop pattern color and continue around in ground color.

Rnd B

1. When you come to the motif, the pattern yarn will be on left side.

2. Work motif stitches by knitting ground stitches and slipping pattern stitches (slipping as if to purl).

3. Knit 1 stitch beyond the motif with ground yarn. Drop ground. Turn.

4. Pick up pattern yarn under, then over, ground yarn. Purl slipped stitches and slip ground stitches.
   When you reach the end of the motif stitches, drop pattern. Turn.

5. Slip motif stitches from left to right needle point. Pick up ground yarn. Knit around.

Continue to alternate these two rows.

On Rnd A, pick up pattern yarn under, then over ground yarn
when necessary to avoid a hole.

I made these mittens with the creature facing away
from the thumb. I believe that was a mistake, so I
have marked the charts for the right and left hands
to face the creature toward the thumb. If you want
it the way I did it, reverse the right and left charts.

These mittens could equally well be done with an invisible thumb since they have only a 2-stitch band. I've reversed the colors on the second mitten but that's certainly not necessary.

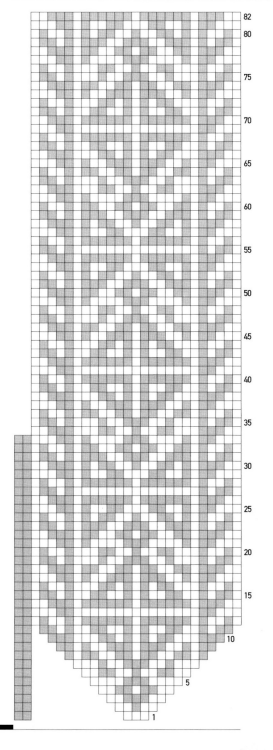

MITTEN

Follow General Directions for Sore-Thumb Mitten. To start the thumb, however, use Striped Band cast-on, casting on 6 sts. When you come to the insertion of the thumb, use 1 mitten st on each side of the band to attach to the thumb. On the first rnd add 1 st on each side of the thumb to restore the pattern. Work through row 54 of Mitten chart and to top of thumb chart. Omit wrist shaping.

CUFF

Additional yarns **50 yds each of C and D**

Chart: Work chart rows 55–82 with **C** on **D** ground.

Edging: With **B**, work attached I-cord edge.

THUMB

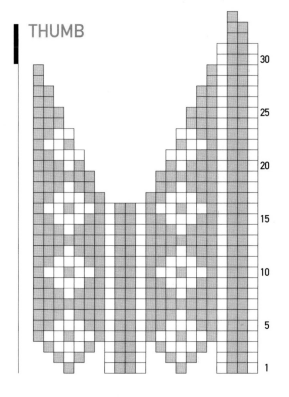

COLORS

A Green

B Purple

C Tan

D Red

Here is a pair of macho mittens in a man's size. They could be made a woman's size by dropping the 2 background stitches on either side of the pattern and changing the band stitches to background color. Because a sore thumb does not work well with a 2-stitch band, it would be better to make an invisible thumb on the woman's mittens.

This pattern is one of my favorites. It's a delight to work, with no long carries in awkward places. (The only long carries are in the heart of the main motif where there are contrast color stitches to catch the yarn behind.) It looks fancy, but it is easy enough so that one is not chained to the chart.

MITTEN

Follow General Directions for Sore-Thumb Mitten. When it comes to the thumb insertion, use 6 sts for the band instead of 2. When shaping the wrist, decrease to 52 stitches with **A**. Work to top of Mitten and Thumb charts.

CUFF

Additional yarns **30 yds C**

Chart: Work rnds 1–4 in chart pat with **C** on **A** ground. Work rnds 5–18 with **C** on **B** ground.

Edging: With **A**, work 4 rnds k1b, p1 rib. Work tubular bind-off.

This is a fine cuff to use for any short mitten instead of ribbing. Since the pattern is a 4-st repeat, it fits easily into other sizes (here, most often, 44 sts).

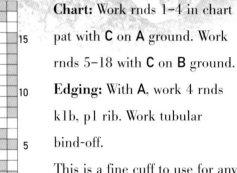

4-st repeat

THUMB

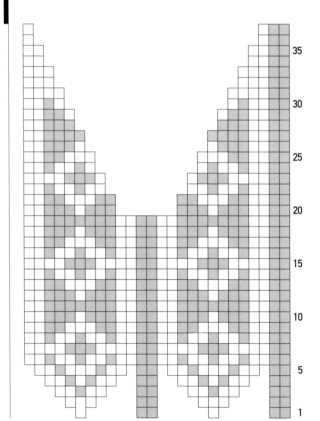

COLORS

A Black

B Green

C Red

This mitten is a good example of a wider band working well on sore-thumb mittens. The possibilities for 5-stitch bands are many (see a few others at top of next page). They do not work well with an invisible thumb because the thumb would have to be inserted in the middle of the band for the mitten to fit. So if you want a band 5 stitches or wider, you most likely want to make sore thumbs.

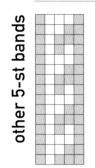
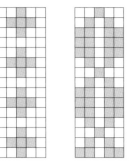
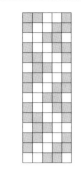

other 5-st bands

MITTEN

Follow General Directions
for Sore-Thumb Mitten.
Work to top of Mitten and
Thumb charts, reversing
colors on second mitten.

THUMB

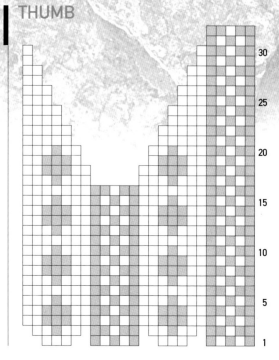

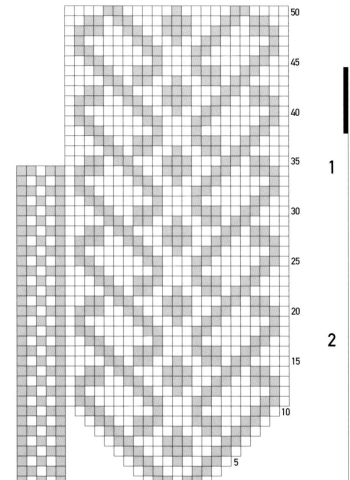

CUFF

Additional yarns

40 yds C; 65 yds each of D and E

1

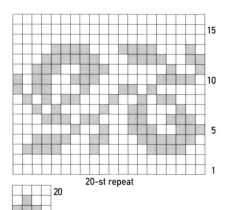

20-st repeat

2

4-st repeat

Work ridge: Rnds 1-2 With **C**, k 1 rnd, p 1 rnd.
Rnd 3 With **B**, *k1, sl 1 with yarn in back (wyib);
rep from*. **Rnd 4** With **B**, *p1, sl 1 wyib; rep
from*. **Rnds 5–6** With **C**, k 1 rnd, p 1 rnd.
With **D**, k 1 rnd, inc to 80 sts as foll: *K2, [BL1,
k1] 18 times, k2; rep from*.

Chart 1: Work 16 rnds of chart with **D** on **E** ground.

Work ridge: Rep rnds 1–6 on 80 sts.

With **E**, k 1 rnd, inc to 100 sts as foll: *K4, BL1; rep from*.

Chart 2: Work 20 rnds of chart with **A**, **B**, **A**, and **D** on

E ground.

Work ridge: Rep rnds 1–6 on 100 sts.

Edging: With **A**, work picot edge.

COLORS

A Dark orange

B Gold

C Purple

D Yellow

E Green

Here is a pair
of mittens for the kind
of grandchild that
inspires them. The beads
undermine the advantage
sore-thumb mittens have
of being able to be worn
on either hand. But I
think the pleasure they
give makes up for the
inconvenience.

These will take half the
yarn of full-sized mittens.

MITTEN

Follow General Directions for Sore-Thumb Mitten. Work to top of Mitten and Thumb charts. You will need 20 small (3mm) silver beads for back of hand. Before beginning, string 10 beads on **B**. Work these beads into the back of the mitten only (not the palm) where indicated on the chart. When shaping wrist, decrease on chart row 33 to 34 sts.

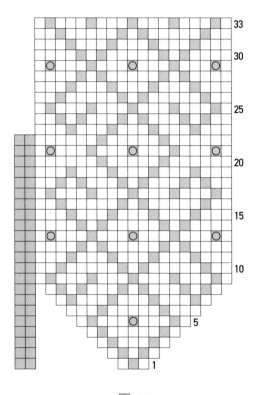

○ Knit in bead

CUFF

Additional yarns **45 yds of C**

Work k1b, p1 rib: 3 rnds **C**, 2 rnds **B**.

Inc to 68 sts as foll: *K1**C**, BL1**A**; rep from*.

Chart: Work 24 rnds of chart, using **A** on **C** ground for rnds 1–8 and **B** on **C** ground for rnds 9–24.

Edging: With **A**, work picot edge.

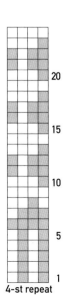

4-st repeat

THUMB

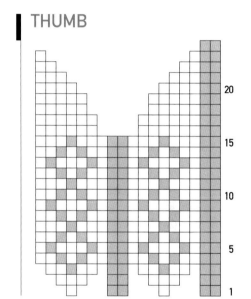

COLORS

A Light blue

B Red

C Green

The band on these mittens is turned to run up the back of the hand and down the palm. This is accomplished by simply placing the thumb in the middle of the body of the mitten. This design is most suitable for sore-thumb mittens. If you made them like invisible-thumb mittens, the pattern would overlap onto the band and look, I think, quite odd.

MITTEN

Follow General Directions for Sore-Thumb Mitten, but cast on 9 sts for mitten (4 sts **B**, 1**A**, 4**B**) and, since there is no thumb band, start the thumb as for Invisible-Thumb Mitten. Work to top of Mitten and Thumb charts.

THUMB

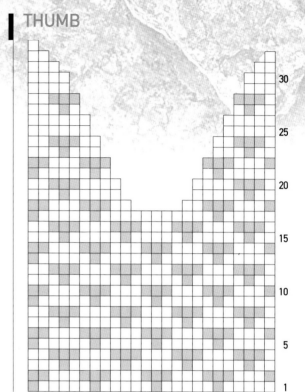

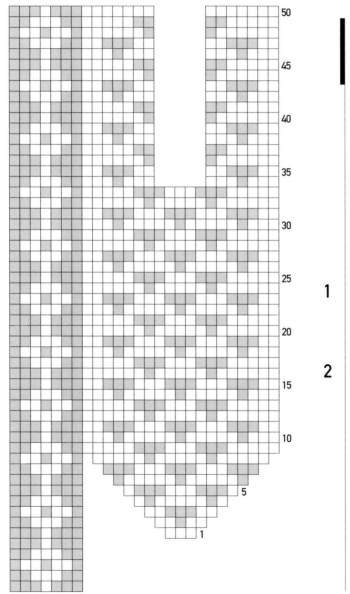

CUFF

Additional yarns

50g **D**; 50 yds **C**; 30 yds **E**

Work k1b, p1 rib: 5 rnds **D**.

With **C**, k 1 rnd, inc to 64 sts as foll:
K2, [BL1, k2] 10 times; rep from.

Chart 1: Work 6 rnds of chart with **E** on **C** ground.

With **D**, k 1 rnd, inc to 84 sts as foll:
K2, [BL1, k3] 10 times; rep from.

1

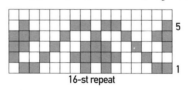

16-st repeat

2

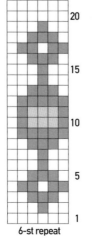

6-st repeat

Chart 2: Work chart rows 1–19 with **B** and **C** on **D** ground. With **D**, work last 2 chart rows, inc to 90 sts on chart row 20 as foll: *BL1, k14; rep from*.

Chart 1: Rep chart 1 with **E** on **C** ground.

Edging: With **D**, work fringe edge.

Embellish: Using photo as guide, work double cross st with **A** and **C**.

Like the preceding mitten, the band here goes over the top. The hand pattern is such, however, that it makes a band along the sides and thumb. This is the band that is used in beginning the thumb.

MITTEN

Follow the General Directions for Sore-Thumb Mitten, figure-8 wrapping 9 sts in **B**. Work across first row of the band chart and when you add **A**, leave a 6" tail. Purl the second row of band chart. Rotate the needles and tighten the sts, then purl first row of the band chart, using the **A** tail for the **A** st. Turn. Knit second row of the band chart using **A** tail. Now pick up 3 sts on the side of the rectangle in pattern, still using **A** tail. Work across the band sts using **A** and drop the tail. Pick up on the other side of the rectangle and continue on. Using photo as guide, alternate **B** and **C**. The thumb begins with a Striped Band. Begin picking up 1 st on the sides after 2 rows. Work to top of Mitten and Thumb charts.

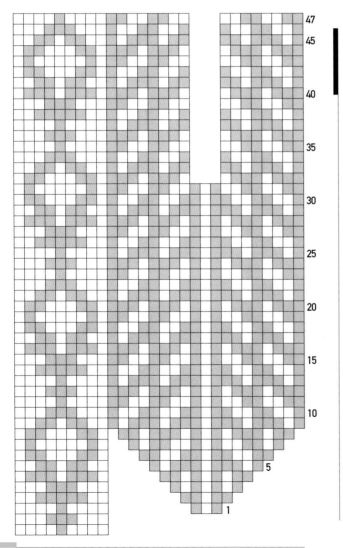

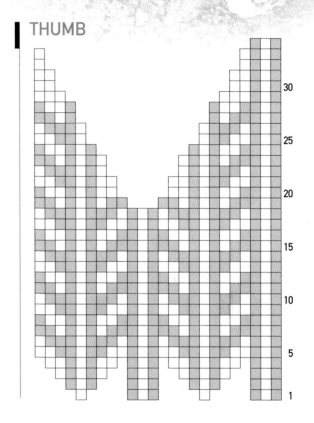

THUMB

CUFF

Additional yarns **60 yds C**; **50g D**; **32 yds each of E and F**

To make bobble (MB): K1, yo, k1, yo, k1 in one st. Turn. Sl 1, k4, turn. Sl 1, p4, turn. Sl 1, k4. Pass the 2nd, then the 3rd, 4th and 5th st over the first. Turn. K 1.

Work k1b, p1 rib: 7 rnds **B**. With **D**, k 2 rnds, inc to 64 sts on first rnd as foll: *K2, [BL1, k2] 10 times; rep from*.

Cut 4 long strands or wind bobbins of **E** and **F**. Use a separate strand for each bobble.

Make bobbles: Next rnd: *K7D, MB **E**, k7D, MB **F**; rep from*.

With **D, k 6 rnds. On next rnd, work bobbles, inc 1 st in **D** between each bobble. Rep from**, keeping the bobbles in line and continuing to inc 1 st in **D**, until there are 7 rows of bobbles. K 1 rnd **D**.

Edging: With **A**, work roll edge.

COLORS

A Light blue

B Dark red

C Purple

D Blue

E Orange

F Violet

These funny looking things are the result of a promise I made to someone who wanted mittens with an index finger. They fit well but are fussier to make than I enjoy. Glove knitters, however, should find them no trouble.

MITTEN

Follow General Directions for Sore-Thumb Mitten. Make the large section to the end of the band and put it aside. Make the index finger and join it to the large section as though it were a thumb. Work around both sections until you reach the thumb join—that is, to the end of the band on the index finger. Work to top of Mitten and Thumb charts.

THUMB

INDEX FINGER   LARGE SECTION

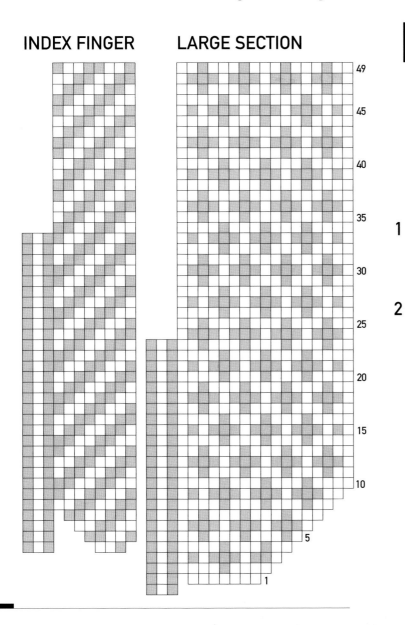

CUFF

Additional yarns **50g A; 70 yds C**

Work k1b, p1 rib: 6 rnds **A**.

With **A**, k 2 rnds, inc to 60 sts on first rnd as foll: *K6, [M1, k2] 8 times; rep from*.

Chart 1: With **C** on **A** ground, work 2 chart rows.

With **A**, k 2 rnds, inc to 88 sts on first rnd as foll: *K2, [M1, k2] 14 times; rep from*.

2-st repeat

Chart 2: Work chart rows 1–21 with **C** on **A** ground. Work to top of chart with **B** on **A** ground.

Edging: With **A** and **C**, work braid edge.

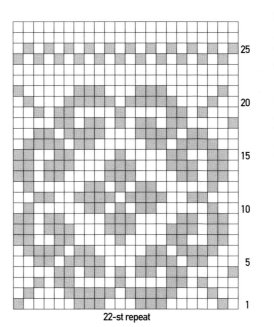

22-st repeat

COLORS

A Purple

B Light aqua

C Red

A gesture here to the tradition, largely Icelandic, of the two-thumbed mitten. They were, and are, made for fishermen for rough work. The second thumb may be a hedge against the thumb's wearing out first, or it may aid in putting them on quickly. Two-thumbed mittens invite design experiments, but I can't believe deeply in their practicality. I made them short because I liked the proportions. They look to me like bizarre cacti.

Perhaps it should be noted that any mittens could be made with double thumbs—just put them in on both sides.

MITTEN

Follow General Directions for Sore-Thumb Mitten, but only figure-8 wrap 3 sts. Begin the thumb the same way, but use **D** instead of **A**. Work to top of Mitten and Thumb charts, changing ground color to **C** between the dotted lines. When shaping wrist, decrease to 40 sts.

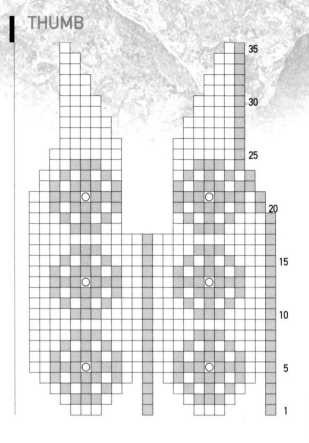

THUMB

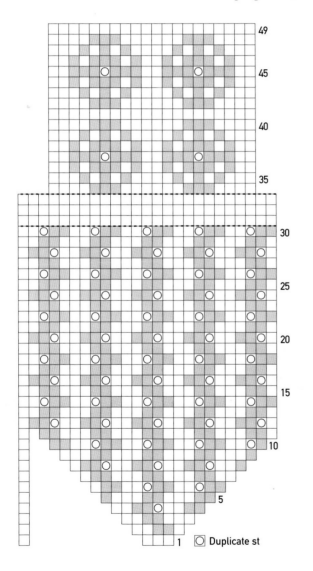

O Duplicate st

CUFF

Additional yarns **50g C (used in mitten);**
30 yds D (used in mitten and cuff)

Work k1b, p1 rib: 13 rnds **D**. Work tubular bind-off.

Embellish: Work duplicate st in **C** where indicated on chart.

COLORS

A Green

B Yellow

C Red

D Turquoise

These are arranged more or less in order of difficulty.

ROLL

Knit 1 rnd.

Purl 3 rnds.

Bind off purlwise.

PICOT

Multiple of 3 sts.

[K1, return st to LH needle] 3 times; k1. Pick up st at the base of the chain just made and bind off the picot st and 2 more sts; rep from.

DOUBLE ROLL

Knit 1 rnd. Purl 3 rnds.

Knit 2 rnds. Purl 3 rnds.

Bind off purlwise.

WOOL BEADS

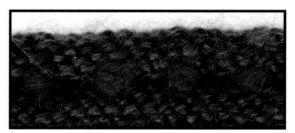

Multiple of 6 sts. Main color (MC), contrast color (CC)

Rnds 1–3 With MC, k 1 rnd, p 2 rnds. **Rnd 4** *With CC, k1, p1, k1 in next stitch; k3 with MC; rep from*. **Rnd 5** *With CC, p3tog, k3 with MC; rep from*. **Rnd 6** With MC, knit. **Rnd 7** With MC, purl. With MC, bind off purlwise.

BRAID

Multiple of 2 sts.

Rnd 1 *K1A, k1B; rep from*. Wrap the next st: Sl st to RH needle, bring both yarns forward, replace sl st on LH needle. Turn knitting so wrong side is facing.

Rnd 2 *(The first st to work should be color **B**.) Pull out a yard or two of each yarn before you start to knit this rnd. K1B. *Pick up **A** under **B** and k1A; pick up **B** under **A** and k1A; rep from* around. The yarns will be twisting around each other as you work, which is why you pulled out the yarn when you started the rnd.

Rnd 3 *Pick up **B** over **A** and k1B; pick up **A** over **B** and k1A; repeat from* around. The yarns will be untwisting as you work this rnd. End by wrapping as before. Turn so right side faces. There's your braid. Bind off, knitting 1**A**, 1**B** around.

---

wrapping loops for fringe

FRINGE

This edging takes more yarn than one could have imagined possible—about 18 yards per mitten.

With fringe color, k 3 rnds.

Rnd 1 *Insert the needle in the next stitch; wrap yarn 3 times around left index finger (see drawing, lower left); grab the loops on the index finger with the needle; pull them through the stitch. Rep from*.

Rnd 2 Knit around, knitting each cluster of loops on the needle as one stitch. Be very careful not to pull the loops all the way through; there is no way to get them back in place, at least none that I have discovered. And the fringe rnd is slow enough to do that no one wants to have to take it out and do it over.

Rnd 3 Knit.

Rnd 4 Bind off.

When you have bound off you should tighten the fringe. You will see that it is composed of pairs of loops (instead of the triads you might have expected). Insert a needle into each of these pairs and pull them up tight. Here, too, be very careful not to make a mistake and pull out one loop. There's no getting it back, though if you're determined you can fake it with a crochet hook and an extra piece of yarn to hold it in.

ATTACHED I-CORD

Cast on 3 sts on LH needle. With an extra needle, k these 3 sts and sl them back onto the LH needle. *K2, ssk (working last I-cord st with st from cuff); sl the 3 sts on RH needle onto LH needle; rep from* around. Leave last 3 sts on RH needle. Cut yarn, leaving a 6" tail. Graft the remaining sts to the cast-on sts.

ATTACHED I-CORD WITH LOOP AND BUTTON

For loop edge Work as for attached I-cord but when you come to the end of the cuff sts, *sl the 3 sts onto LH needle. Knit them with RH needle. Rep from* 10 times. Replace sts on LH needle and graft them to the cast-on sts.

For button edge Work as for loop edge but before grafting, tie the 10-row I-cord in a knot.

ATTACHED DOUBLE I-CORD

Work one attached I-cord edge and graft ends together. With same or another color, pick up 1 st for every row in the 2nd (middle) st of I-cord. K 1 rnd on these sts. Work I-cord as before.

Attached I-cord and these two variations were introduced to us by Elizabeth Zimmermann and Meg Swansen.

FAT BEADED FRINGE

This is not an edging that you will want to undertake if you have an aversion to dealing with ends. There are 132 to dispose of.

But if this is not a consideration:

Multiple of 3 sts.

Work 5 rows of I-cord on 3 sts as foll: [K3, sl sts to LH needle] 5 times. Cut yarn and run end through sts. String bead on yarn. Run yarn into I-cord and fasten off. (Beads can be omitted, of course.)

LOOPED I-CORD

This is another edging with many ends. It's a little easier to deal with than the fat fringe because the I-cord loops are long enough to run both ends into.

Multiple of 12 sts.

Work 11 rows of I-cord on 3 sts as foll: [K3, sl sts to LH needle] 11 times. Skip the next 6 sts and graft the I-cord to the next 3 sts. Work 11 rows of I-cord on what are now the first 3 sts of the rnd. Run this I-cord over the first loop made, skip the next 3 sts and graft the I-cord to the following 3 sts. In same way, *work 11 rows of I-cord on the skipped 3 sts, run the I-cord over the previous loop, skip the next 3 sts and graft the I-cord to the following 3 sts; rep from* around. Graft the final I-cord loop to the first set of 3 sts that were skipped.

BALL FRINGE

Multiple of 4 sts.

Rnd 1 *K2**A**, k2**B**; rep from*. **Rnds 2–5** *K2**A**, p2**B**; rep from*.

Rnd 6 Bind off as foll: K1**A**, k1**B**, pass **A** st over **B** st; *work bobble in next st with **B**, pass **B** st over bobble st; k1**A**, pass bobble st over **A** st; k1**A**, pass **A** st over; k1**B**, pass **A** st over; rep from*.

To make bobble K1, yo, k1, yo, k1 in one st. Turn. Sl 1, k4, turn. Sl 1, p4, turn. Sl 1, k4. Pass the 2nd, 3rd, 4th, then 5th st over the first st and off the needle. Turn. K1.

Those who have learned to make bobbles with reverse knitting (knitting left to right) might like to try reverse purling (purling left to right) for these bobbles. It isn't hard and purled bobbles look so fine.

---

purling left to right

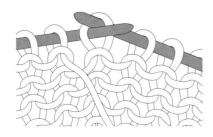

1. Enter back loop with left needle.

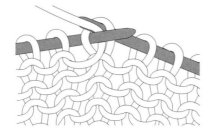

2. Wrap yarn from right to left over left needle.

3. Draw wrap through and onto left needle to form new stitch.

After making a magnificent pair of mittens, I assume you will both want to line them and want to line them as quickly and easily as possible. The directions that follow try to satisfy these desires while making linings of the highest quality. It is not necessary to knit a whole second pair of finely crafted mittens, but it is necessary to produce two mittens in a looser gauge.

I always line my mittens with Angora. Not the finest longest-haired French Angora. To the contrary. I keep my eyes open for inferior Angora and Angora blends. There's no question that Angora makes the most sensuous and warm lining. If it isn't available, the next best choice is either alpaca or kid mohair. (Do not use fluffy acrylic, however nice it feels. It will not keep your hands warm in cold weather and it will not be warm when wet.) Any of these choices will knit up nicely at about 4½ stitches to the inch.

It is a matter of personal preference whether you want to knit the lining attached to the mitten or separate from it. If you knit it attached, the mitten is hanging down while you're working, but you don't have to sew it in when you're done. You begin by turning back the cuff and picking up 40 stitches in the purl bumps before the wrist (see photo, lower left). Follow directions for circular knitting and when done run any ends inside and push the lining up into the mitten. It's neat. It's done.

On the other hand, if you are going to make the lining separately, you might even consider doing it flat instead of round—it all depends on how much you like working with double pointed needles. A seam will never show on the inside and if by chance you have a bulky knitting machine, the lining can be worked up in no time flat.

So here follow directions for both circular knit linings and flat knit linings.

For invisible-thumb mittens

Circular knit

Cast on 40 sts and leave an 8-10" tail to sew the lining in with. Knit around about 2½", the length from wrist to thumb juncture. Place 8 sts on hold. Cast on 8 sts over those on hold and continue knitting until the piece measures ¾" less than the finished mitten. *K1, k2tog; rep from*, end k1. Knit 1 rnd. K2tog around. Cut yarn and pull end through remaining sts.

For the thumb, pick up 8 sts where they were cast on and slip the sts on hold onto 2 needles. Pick up an extra st in each corner. Knit around until almost thumb length. Then k2tog around, cut yarn, and pull the end through the remaining sts.

Flat knit (and machine)

Cast on 40 sts and work back and forth in stockinette st to the thumb juncture (approximately 2½"). Place 8 sts on hold. On the next row cast on 8 sts over those on hold. Work until ¾" from tip of mitten. *K1, k2tog; rep from*, end k1. Purl back. K2tog across. Cut yarn leaving an 8-10" tail, and pull the tail through the sts.

On one needle, place the 8 sts on hold, pick up 1 st in space before cast-on, pick up 8 sts in cast-on edge. Purl back and continue in stockinette st until just short of thumb length. K2tog across row, cut yarn and pull through remaining sts.

Sew down the side of the thumb with the thumb tail. Sew down the side of the mitten with the tip tail. Turn the lining inside out. Put it on and put your hand into the mitten. Withdraw your hand, leaving the lining in place. With the cast-on tail, sew lining to the wrist. Run all ends into the space between lining and mitten.

When doing this on a knitting machine, you may want to move onto knitting needles for the decreasing.

For sore-thumb mittens

The method is the same as for invisible-thumb mittens, but you will have to shape a thumb gusset.

Circular knit

Cast on 40 sts. Knit around. At thumb side, *M1, k2, M1 every other rnd.

After about 2½", when you reach the thumb juncture, put all sts between and including increases, on an extra piece of yarn. Cast on 2 sts over the sts on hold. Continue knitting.

Finish as for invisible-thumb mittens.

Flat knit

Cast on 40 sts. Purl back. Increase at beginning of every knit row as follows: K1, M1, k2, M1. (For the other mitten, inc at beg of every purl row as follows: P1, M1, p2, M1.) Continue in stockinette st until you reach the thumb juncture. Put all sts between and including increases on an extra piece of yarn. Cast on 2 sts over removed sts. Finish as for invisible-thumb mittens.

On these drawings, the black arrow starts at the needle or

yarn (whichever is moving) and outlines the path it will take.

KNITTING TECHNIQUES

3-needle bind-off

Place right sides together. *K2tog (one from front needle and one from back needle). Rep from* once. Bind first stitch off over 2nd stitch. Continue to k2tog (1 front stitch and 1 back stitch) and bind off across.

stringing beads

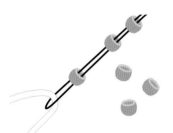

Using a loop of thread or fine wire, string required number of beads on yarn.

knitting-in beads

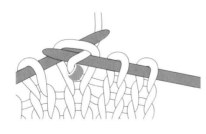

Slip bead up to back of work. As you knit the stitch, push bead through to front of work.

stockinette graft

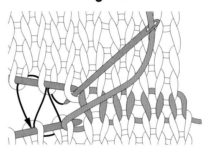

1. Arrange stitches on two needles.

2. Thread a blunt needle with matching yarn (approximately 1" per stitch).

3. Working from right to left, with right sides facing you, begin with steps 3a and 3b:

    a. *Front needle:* yarn through first stitch as if to purl, leave stitch on needle.

    b. *Back needle:* yarn through first stitch as if to knit, leave on needle.

4. Work 4a and 4b across:

    a. *Front needle:* through first stitch as if to knit, slip off needle: through next stitch as if to purl, leave on needle.

    b. *Back needle:* through first stitch as if to purl, slip off needle: through next stitch as if to knit, leave on needle.

5. Adjust tension to match rest of knitting.

knit left to right

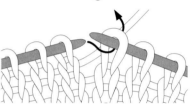

1. Enter back loop with left needle.

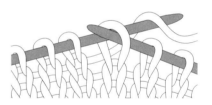

2. Wrap yarn from left to right over left needle.

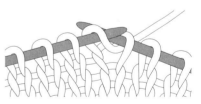

3. Draw wrap through and onto left needle to form new stitch.

Note I find it easier to wrap the yarn the "wrong" way in Step 2 and compensate by knitting the stitches in the back loop on the return row.

sl2-k1-p2sso

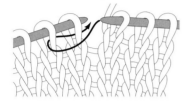

1. Slip 2 stitches together to right needle as if to knit.

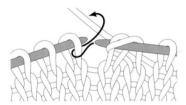

2. Knit next stitch.

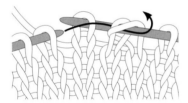

3. Pass 2 slipped stitches over knit stitch and off right needle.

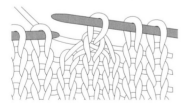

4. Completed: 3 stitches become 1; the center stitch is on top.

ssk

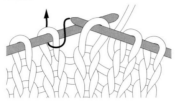

1. Slip 2 stitches one at a time to right needle, slipping as if to knit.

2. Knit these 2 stitches together by slipping left needle into them through the front from left to right.

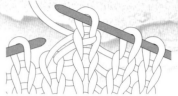

3. Knit together with right needle.

make 1 (M1)

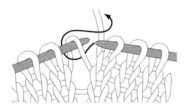

1. With right needle from back of work, pick up strand between last st knitted and next st. Place on left needle and knit, twisting the strand by working into the loop at the back of the needle.

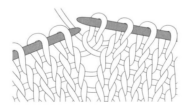

2. This is the completed increase.

backward loop increase (BL1)

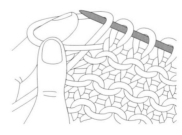

To increase between stitches, form a backward loop on right-hand needle. Knit the loop in the next row.

lifted increase

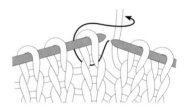

1. Knit into the purl bump behind the next stitch on the left-hand needle.

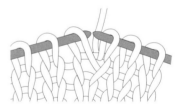

2. Lifted increase complete. Knit the next stitch and continue.

Note: In this book, M1 means use *either* the make 1 increase or the backward loop increase, BL1 means work *only* the backward loop increase illustrated above.

tubular bind-off

A rounded rib bind-off is, essentially, grafting the knit stitches to the purl stitches. To see what you are doing before following the illustrated directions, try this: separate 20 k1, p1 rib stitches on 2 dpn so that 10 knit stitches are on one, and 10 purl stitches are on the other. Hold purl needle behind knit needle and graft stitches together.

This method produces an invisibly secured edge. The ribs flow smoothly from RS to WS. Thread a blunt needle with matching yarn. Assuming the first st on left-hand needle is a knit stitch, bring yarn through first stitch as if to purl, leave stitch on needle.

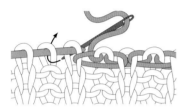

1. Take needle behind knit stitch, between first 2 stitches, and through purl stitch as if to knit. Leave stitches on needle.

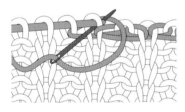

2. Bring yarn to front, then through knit stitch as if to knit and slip stitch off needle.

3. Take needle in front of purl stitch and through knit stitch as if to purl. Leave stitches on needle.

4. Bring yarn through purl stitch as if to purl and slip off needle.

5. Even out tension. Repeat Steps 1-4.

weaving in carries

Uses
Carries over more than 5 stitches should be woven in. This is easiest when the working yarn is in the right hand.

Bring the left-hand yarn over right needle and knit a stitch: slip left-hand yarn off and knit next stitch.

EMBROIDERY TECHNIQUES

stem or outline stitch

1. Actually the 'wrong side' of Back stitch. Great for curves; makes a raised line.

duplicate stitch

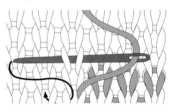

Duplicate stitch (also known as Swiss darning) is just that: with a blunt tapestry needle threaded with contrast color yarn, cover a knit stitch with an embroidered stitch of the same shape.

Palestrina knot

A

B

C

D

Algerian eye

Double cross   Smyrna cross

ABBR.

b	in back of stitch
BL1	backward loop increase
CC	contrast color
dec	decreas(e)(ed)(es)(ing)
dpn	double pointed needle(s)
g	gram(s)
"	inch(es)
inc	increas(e)(ed)(es)(ing)
k	knit(ted)(ing)(s)
LH	left hand
M1	make one increase
MC	main color
p	purl(ed)(ing)(s)
psso	pass slipped stitch(es) over
rep	repeat(s)
RH	right hand
rnd	round(s)
sl	slip(ped)(ping)
st(s)	stitch(es)
tog	together
wyib	with yarn in back
yd	yard(s)
yo	yarn over

I use Washfast Acid dyes from Pro Chemical and Dye Co. P.O. Box 14, Somerset, MA, 02726. I find them consistent, available, and extremely easy to use.

The toner referred to in some of the dye recipes is composed of .5g490+2g351+6g119. Those are the amounts I shake together at one time. The proportions are 1:4:12. The toner lasts well in powdered form but changes color in a few days when dissolved. It's only trustworthy when freshly mixed.

4-1
A Green 728 1%
B Yellow 119 & 817 25:1 .5%
C Black 672 3%
D Purple 338 & 817 1:1 .125%
E Red 338 1%

4-2
A Dark green 725 & 672 2:1 1%
B Blue 725 .125%
C White washed, undyed
D Purple 338 & 490 3:1 .5%
E Pink 338 & 817 15:1 .5%

4-3
A Dark green 725 & 490 2:1 2%
B Pink 370 & 817 10:1 2%
C Purple 370 & 817 7:1 2%
D Light green 728 2%
E Orange 351 & toner 1:1 1%
   (see note on dyes for toner recipe)

4-4
A Purple 338 & 490 3:1 1%
B Red 338 2%
C Blue green 725 & 490 2:1 2%
D Yellow 119 & 817 50:1 .5%

4-5
A Black 672 3%
B White washed unbleached wool

4-6
A White washed, undyed
B Green 728 2%
C Blue 425c & 338 3:1 .5%
D Violet 370 & 817 7:1 2%

4-7
A Purple 370 & 817 10:1 2%
B Red 338 2%
C Green 728 2%
D Violet 370 & 817 7:1 2%

4-8
A Black 672 3%
B Violet 370 & 817 7:1 2%
C Orange 351 & toner 1:1 1%

4-9
A Coral 351 & toner 1:1 .125%
B Red 349 & 817 20:1 3%
C Purple 338 & 490 3:1 1%
D Green 728 2%

4-10
A Red 349 & 817 20:1 2%
B Gold 135 & toner 3:1 2%
C Purple 338 & 490 3:1 2%
D Black 672 3%
E Green 119 & 672 1:1 1%

4-11
A Tan 503 & 135 1:1 1%
B Orange 351 & toner 1:1 1%
C Green 119 & 672 1:1 1%
Seven assorted scraps

4-12
A Black 672 3%
B Tan 503 & 135 1:1 .35%
C Green 672 & 119 1:1 2%
D Orange 351 & toner 1:1 1%

4-13
A Tan 503 & 135 1:1 .35%
B Mud green 672 & 119 1:1 2%
C Blue green 725 & 490 2:1 2%
D Purple 338 & 490 3:1 1%

4-14
A Black 672 3%
B Blue 725 & 490 2:1 2%
C Purple 338 & 490 3:1 1%
D Green 672 & 119 1:1 1%
E Yellow 119 & 817 25:1 .5%

4-15
A Tan 233 & 728 1:1 .25%
B Small amounts (at least 6 yards each) of bright colors over-dyed with .25% 502

5-1
A Blue 478 & 725 1:1 1%
B Pink 338 & 817 10:1 1%
C Green 728 & 119 1:1 1%
D Orange 135 & 366 2:1 1%

5-2
A Violet 370 & 817 7:1 2%
B Orange 351 & toner 1:1 1%
C Magenta 338 & 817 10:1 1%
D Green 728 2%
E Chartreuse 119 & 728 30:1 2%
F Blue 818 .5%

5-3
A Dark green 725 & 672 2:1 2%
B Light green 728 & 199c 1:1 1%
C Gold 119 & toner 3:1 1%
D Blue 478 & 725 1:1 1%
E Purple 338 & 817 1:1 1%
F Red 351 & toner 3:1 2%
G Pink 370 & 817 10:1 1%

5-4
A Green 725 & 490 2:1 2%
B Purple 338 & 490 3:1 1%
C Orange 351 & toner 1:1 .25%
D Yellow 119 & 199c 1:1 .5%

5-5
A Magenta 338 & 817 10:1 1%
B Yellow 199c & 119 1:1 .5%
C Green 725 & 490 2:1 2%
D Violet 370 & 817 7:1 2%
E Black 672 3%

5-6
A Purple 338 & 425 3:1 1%
B Light orange 135 & 366 2:1 1%
C Dark orange 351 & toner 1:1 1%

5-7
A Green 503 & 725 2:1 1%
B Yellow 199c .03125%
C Orange 135 & 366 2:1 1%
D Purple 338 & 425 3:1 1%

5-8
A Purple 817 & 338 1:1 1%
B Blue 478 & 725 1:1 1%
C Green 490 & 135 3:10 .5%

5-9
A White natural, washed
B Pink 338 & 490 3:2 .25%
C Blue 728 & 817 2:1 .5%

5-10
A Green 503 & 725 2:1 1%
B Pink 338 & 817 10:1 1%
C Orange 135 & 366 2:1 1%
D Purple 338 & 425 3:1 1%

5-11
A Pale green 503 & 135 1:1 .25%
B Pink 351 & 672 2:1 .125%
C Medium green 233 & 728 & 490 10:10:1 .5%

5-12
A Blue 728 & 817 2:1 2%
B Tan 233 & 728 1:1 .25%
C Dark tan 233 & 728 & 490 10:10:1 .5%
D Red 349 & 817 10:1 2%
E Dark green 725 & 672 2:1 2%
F Purple 338 & 425 3:1 1%

5-13
A Purple 817 & 338 1:1 1%
B Green 728 & 199c 1:1 1%
C Tan 503 & 135 1:1 .35%
D Orange 351 & toner 1:1 1%
E Pink 338 & 817 10:1 1%

5-14
A Gold 119 & toner 3:1 2%
B Red 349 & 817 10:1 2%
C Purple 338 & 425 3:1 1%
D Black 672 3%

5-15
A Dark green 725 & 672 2:1 2%
B Purple 817 & 338 1:1 1%
C Rust 351 & toner 1:1 2%
D Light green 728 & 199c 1:1 1%
E Pink 351 & 672 2:1 .125%

5-16
A Light blue 725 .03125%
B Pink 338 & 817 10:1 1%
C Purple 338 & 425 3:1 1%

5-17
A Green 440 & Toner 3:1 .5%
B Yellow 199c & 487 2:1 .03125%
C Purple 425 & 338 1:3 .25%

6-1
A Red 349 & 817 10:1 2%
B Light green 728 & 199c 1:1 1%
C Dark green 725 & 672 2:1

6-2
A Red 349 & 817 10:1 2%
B Purple 338 & 817 1:1 1%
C Blue 728 & 817 2:1 2%
D Orange 351 & toner 1:1 1%
E Green 728 2%

6-3
A Green 233 & 728 & 490 10:10:1 .5%
B Purple 490 & 338 1:3 1%
C Tan 503 & 135 1:1 .35%
D Red 349 & 817 10:1 2%

6-4
A Black 672 3%
B Green 503 & 233 & 490 10:10:1 .5%
C Red 338 & 817 10:1 1%

6-5
A Dark orange 351 & toner 1:1 1%
B Gold 119 & toner 3:1 2%
C Purple 338 & 490 3:1 1%
D Yellow 119 & 199c 1:1 .03125%
E Green 503 & 725 2:1 1%

6-6
A Light blue 725 .03125%
B Red 338 & 817 10:1 1%
C Green 440 & Toner .5%

6-7
A Blue-green 725 & 490 2:1 2%
B Gold 135 & toner 3:1 2%
C Orange 351 & toner 1:1 1%
D Pink 338 & 817 10:1 1%
E Green 728 2%

6-8
A Light blue 725 .03125%
B Dark red 349 & 817 10:1 2%
C Purples 817 & 338 1:1 1%
D Blue 425 & 338 3:1 1%
E Orange 351 & toner 1:1 .5%
F Violet 370 & 817 10:1 2%

6-9
A Purple 338 & 425 3:1 1%
B Light aqua 199c & 487 2:1 .03125%
C Red 338 & 817 10:1 1%

6-10
A Green 728 & 199c 1:1 1%
B Yellow 199c & 119 1:1 .5%
C Red 338 & 817 10:1 1%
D Turquoise 478 2%

It is highly unlikely that many will be moved to dye their own yarn for these mittens, but some may wish to buy kits for particular mittens. Merike Saarniit, who runs Carolina Homespun, will dye the yarn and make up kits for almost all the mittens in this book. Anyone interested should contact her at 1-800-450-SPUN or on the World Wide Web: knittinguniverse.com

general notes

1 Use either a 2-stitch or a 3-stitch band.

2 Begin and end thumb to fit.

3 Lengthen or shorten mitten as needed.

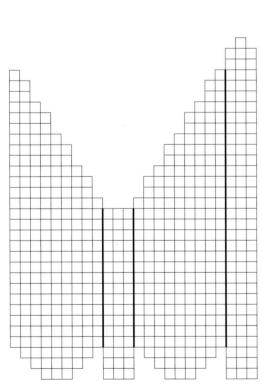

Basic sore thumb

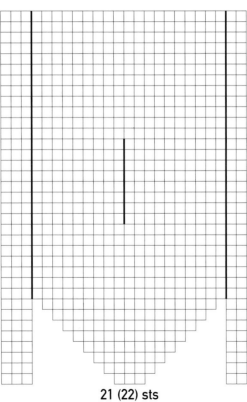

21 (22) sts
Small child's mitten at 6½ sts to 1"

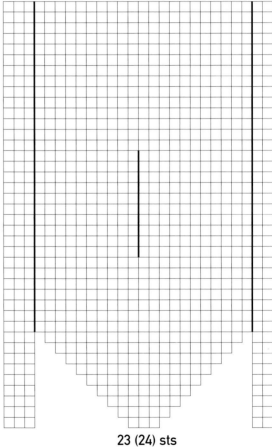

23 (24) sts
Medium child's mitten at 6½ sts to 1"

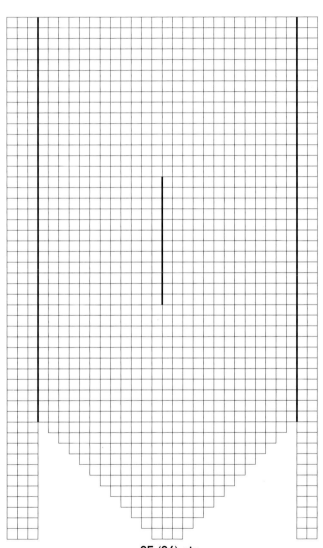

25 (26) sts
Women's mitten at 6$\frac{1}{2}$ sts to 1"

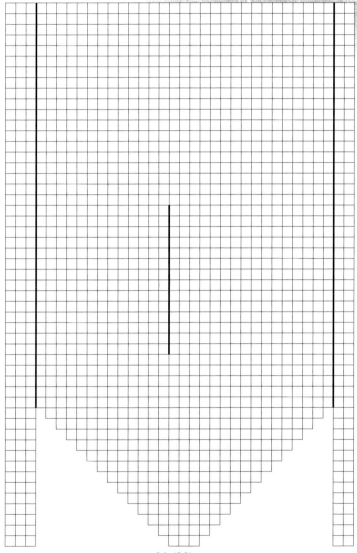

31 (32) sts
Man's mitten at 6$\frac{1}{2}$ sts to 1"

colophon

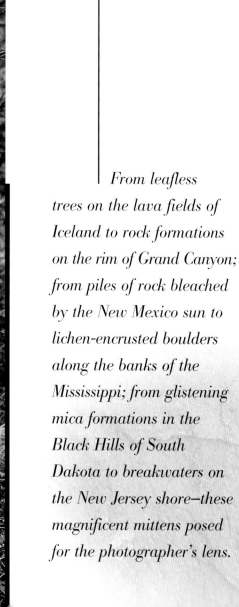

From leafless trees on the lava fields of Iceland to rock formations on the rim of Grand Canyon; from piles of rock bleached by the New Mexico sun to lichen-encrusted boulders along the banks of the Mississippi; from glistening mica formations in the Black Hills of South Dakota to breakwaters on the New Jersey shore—these magnificent mittens posed for the photographer's lens.

Our first impromptu photo shoot took place in Iceland, halfway between Reykjavík and Akarnes where a crystal-clear river meets the sea. Clouds spilled over the jet-black mountain peaks like so many rolls of unspun wool in a black dye pot, reminding me of another far-away stream.

Of a spot in the Peloponnese where my mother would go to dye her wool. Magically, her old copper kettle transformed the rough, hand-sheared-and-spun Balkan skeins into colorful splashes of dripping color. These she placed to dry on the sun-bathed rocks that formed the ravine's walls.

And so the idea came to me—what to do with the bag of mittens we were carrying. *Knitter's* Editor Nancy J. Thomas acted as our impromptu stylist, spreading mittens about the banks and on rocks jutting barely above the water's level. These rocks revealed Iceland's volcanic and to us past appeared as though painted on a dark canvas by an unseen artist to complement Anna's mittens: here one was decorated with pointillist specks, there another brushed in fine white lines.

We were surrounded by mittens: on the cushion of moss and multi-colored lichens that provided an endless soft canvas; on an adjacent clump of dry grass that made a nest for one pair; on a handful of snow sculpted by wind and sun into a perfect frame for another; and on a stark, leaf-less bush that became a mitten tree.

It was late March, and the cold Icelandic wind began to blow harder. *Magnificent Mittens* Editor Elaine Rowley holding a round scrim valiantly tried to act as a windbreak, but we had to stop. Besides, we had a plane to catch in two hours. But not before we said a quick goodbye to our friends at the Tinna yarn shop in picturesque Hafnarfjördur, a sea-side town near Keflavík airport. When the shop owner's son Hugi Hreidarsson and his pretty friend, Bergrós Kjartansdóttir, tried on our mittens, another shoot was soon in progress, this time at a nearby rock garden.

"I confess I was moved to the core by the rocks," Anna said seeing the Chapter Three photographs from Iceland. "I don't have much of a sense of geography, and a rather poor sense of the romance of travel, but the romance of rocks I do feel. I never before thought of rocks as the appropriate background for my mittens. Now I feel definitely that's the way to go: if they're not on peoples' hands, they should be on rocks…"

So it was unanimous. But where does one find more rocks in the middle of the Prairie to photograph the rest of the book? Luckily, a phone call from Australia provided the answer: could I, my sister Anna Diakos wished to know, meet her younger son Costa in San Francisco? I did, and from the plateaus of New Mexico to the Great Plains, Costa and I climbed rock piles like wild goats—to the amusement of passing motorists—with tripod, light meter, scrim, and mittens in hand.

When Costa boarded a plane in New York to catch up with friends in Spain, XRX Marketing Director Benjamin Xenakis took his place and rock climbing was on again. From the huge boulders half-buried in Central Park, to those forming retaining walls at The Cloisters, to others on the Jersey shore, Benjamin and I found enough incredibly beautiful rocks to photograph *Magnificent Mittens* many times over.

Design Director Mark Sampson combined Anna's words and my photographs into a pleasing, unified whole. He chose a classic typeface, Berthold Bodoni Antiqua Light, for the text; Berkeley Old Style for chapter headings, particularly because of its elegant numerals; and DINMittelschrift, a modern typeface that reflects Anna's notion of making mittens a part of modern life.

"These mittens are very dear to me," Anna says as we walk through a clearing at Valley Forge National Park. We have stolen her away from her Stitches teaching schedule long enough to shoot her author's photograph. "I am happy to share them," Anna says, "they do feel like my mittens, so different from any other.

"They came from the Turkish stockings, but I wasn't that interested in knitting a lot of socks—they just get holes in them—and they're in shoes! But when I was making the tip of the toe for a Turkish stocking, it occurred to me that here was a neat technique—and an answer to mittens.

"The Turkish toe made an elegant increase because you arranged the pattern at the tip of the mitten and you worked it from there. You had this band that could go all the way around the mitten. In other words, it integrated the shaping into the design, so it was far more elegant to make. And you could knit the thumb first, separately, put it in as you went down—not have to knit it with the whole mitten hanging from it!—and when you were done you were done! So, you did the hardest part first, the thumb went in on its way, and suddenly mittens became fun to do.

"Also, it was in Lizbeth Upitis' book *Latvian Mittens* [Schoolhouse

Press] that I saw mittens that looked the same, back side and palm side. It seemed to me mysterious when you had this complicated pattern how you figured out your thumb to match—the invisible thumb. Here came an example of the sudden cessation of stupidity: I realized, when I started charting mittens, that I could just draw the thumb on the graph! Then I could make 'invisible-thumb' mittens, which really delighted me.

"So now mittens were fun, but when you got to the wrist they were still just mittens. Someone had talked about long cuffs on mittens as a practical matter, so snow wouldn't get in, so I started making "skirts" for the arms: big cuffs, in patterns that were fun, and they seemed to go very nicely with the shape of the mitten. I had something beautiful to make.

"I couldn't use the patterns I had used in *Fancy Feet* [Lark Books]—knitters don't want to run into the same patterns here!—so I said to myself I've got to make mittens I've never made before, think in ways I've never thought before about patterns and designs. I started playing with graph paper, looking at rugs and Fair Isle patterns.

"Because I had been dyeing yarn for a while, I had big baskets full of little skeins of yarn. When I wanted to make something I'd dig through my baskets and put colors together: 'Let's see what I feel like today…' I would often try seven shades of purple against a rust. And I'd have seven shades of rust, from an orange-rust to a pinky rust, and I would just pair them up and get the combination I wanted and add other things to it. So the color combinations came about from being able to select from *all* the colors. And that's why I put the dye recipes in: anyone who loves color is well advised to gath-

er *all* the colors, because then you have all these options to work with."

From Anna's dyepot, needles, and fingers; from my Hasselblad; from the edge of the Arctic Circle; and from Coast to Coast, we bring you *Magnificent Mittens*.

—*Alexis Yiórgos Xenakis*
SIOUX FALLS, SOUTH DAKOTA

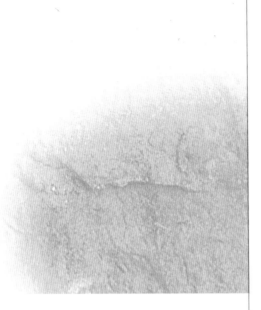

other publications from XRX, Inc.

Ethnic Socks and Stockings

The Great American Afghan

Knitter's Magazine

Weaver's Magazine